Barrow Mead, Bath, 1964

Excavation of a Medieval Peasant House

Jayne Woodhouse

British Archaeological Reports 28
1976

British Archaeological Reports

122 Banbury Road, Oxford OX2 7BP, England

B.A.R. 28, 1976: "Barrow Mead, Bath, 1964: Excavation of a Medieval Peasant House".
© Jayne Woodhouse, 1976.

ISBN 9780904531312 paperback
ISBN 9781407319223 e-book
DOI https://doi.org/10.30861/9780904531312
A catalogue record for this book is available from the British Library
This book is available at www.barpublishing.com

CONTENTS

LIST OF FIGURES

page

LIST OF PLATES

(photographs by P. A. Rahtz)

SUMMARY

Barrow Mead is a complex of medieval buildings and enclosures, probably a hamlet. There was earlier occupation in the Iron Age (Glastonbury culture) and Roman periods, and there were also post-medieval buildings on the site. Although most of the area was destroyed with little record, a medieval house was excavated in 1954, and 1964: the earlier of these explorations is already published. This report deals with the later and fuller investigations. An Iron Age ditch was overlaid by early medieval timber buildings, and then by a sequence of stone structures of the 13th-14th centuries. The latest phase of these is represented by a long house with a wide doorway, later modified to a dwelling house. Finds include Iron Age, Roman and medieval pottery, coins and some metal objects.

INTRODUCTION

The site is situated at ST 729628, two miles SW of Bath, to the north of Wansdyke. The underlying strata are of Cotswold Oolitic limestone, here covered with yellow-green clay which comprises the 'natural' under the archaeological features. The medieval house which is the subject of this report was part of a complex of earthworks observed and partly investigated in advance of destruction by the building of Culverhay School, West Hill, Bath.

In 1954 two days were spent excavating the SE wall of the house and part of the paved yard (Rahtz, 1960-1). A contractor's trench had destroyed some of the interior but this was cleaned back to provide a section (Rahtz, 1960-1, Fig. 5).

In 1964 further excavations were carried out on a part of the site which had been previously covered by a heap of topsoil (T1; layer 1 in sections). Unfortunately in the ten year interval destruction of the interior had continued. An area approximately 53 x 14 ft was excavated, and a smaller trench extended to the NW from this (hereafter called the North-West Trench; Fig. 2). The plan was related to that of the 1954 area by using the west wall of the school gymnasium which appears as a fixed point on both.

This report takes the following form: a description of the earthworks and the documentary evidence is followed by an account of the excavation, and a discussion of the results. The wider implications of Barrow Mead are then discussed in relation to what is known about medieval peasant houses. Finally there is a short discussion on deserted medieval villages in Somerset.

Feet and inches have been used throughout to correspond to the measurements in the original records.

ACKNOWLEDGEMENTS

The excavation was financed by the Ancient Monuments Inspectorate of the (then) Ministry of Public Buildings and Works, (now the Department of the Environment). This report was prepared as part of the requirements for the degree of M. A. in Medieval Archaeology at the University of Birmingham in 1973.

I would like to thank Mr. P. A. Rahtz for placing the finds and records of the excavation at my disposal; Mr. C. C. Dyer for his help with the documentary evidence; Mr. J. G. Hurst and Mr. M. R. McCarthy for their comments on the pottery; Mr. S. E. Ellis, Mr. Ian H. Goodall, and Mr. Alan G. Vince for their specialist reports; and Mr. M. Aston for his additions to, and comments on, the section entitled 'Deserted Medieval Villages in Somerset'.

THE SETTLEMENT

THE EARTHWORKS

The earthworks which formerly existed at Barrow Mead were those of a small settlement of the 13th-14th centuries, and of post-medieval buildings which stood in one part of the site. These were described in some detail in the first report (Rahtz, 1960-1, 64; Fig. 3) and will only be summarised here.

The site was crossed by two hollow ways. The one to the west and south of the site was thought to be the medieval drove road. The other, which wound diagonally across the site, was also thought to be medieval. Two areas of medieval buildings were observed: A to the NE of the hollow way and aligned with it, from which 13th century pottery was recovered; and B which includes the excavated house. There were traces of further buildings to the NW and SE of B, and post-medieval occupation of 17th-18th century date in the west part of the site. Apart from the medieval house described in this report, excavation of the site was confined to a number of trial trenches. ✳

The number of house platforms which were visible suggests that the site was a hamlet or farm rather than a nucleated village: a description which can be applied to many medieval sites in Somerset (see later, p. 28).

There is a further series of house platforms and scarping to the south of the Barrow Mead complex in field 112, and also in Middle Field (Fig. 1) where a medieval dovecote has been excavated (Bolwell, 1957, 169).

DOCUMENTARY EVIDENCE

There is very little documentary evidence for Barrow Mead. All the references are from manorial documents, and only refer indirectly to Barrow Mead. They are concerned solely with land transactions and give no indication of the type of settlement, nor any information concerning the population.

In the first report (Rahtz, 1960-1, 62), the excavator was not clear whether Barrow Mead was to be equated with the documentarily recorded Barewe or Bergh. Barewe however is usually associated with Barrow Gurney, 12 miles to the west, or North and South Barrow, 22 miles to the SW. Bergh is equated with a natural knoll to the west of the site known as High Barrow Hill (K. Quest, 62), and it is probable that Barrow Mead is derived from this. Bergh, Barewe, and Barrow have many derivations which all come from the same source - the Old English beorg meaning "a mountain, hill, hillock, mound" (Ekwall, 1960, 38), hence the possible confusion. Place names can only be associated with a particular settlement when they are clearly linked with a landowner who is known to have connections with the place, or when some indication of the location if given.

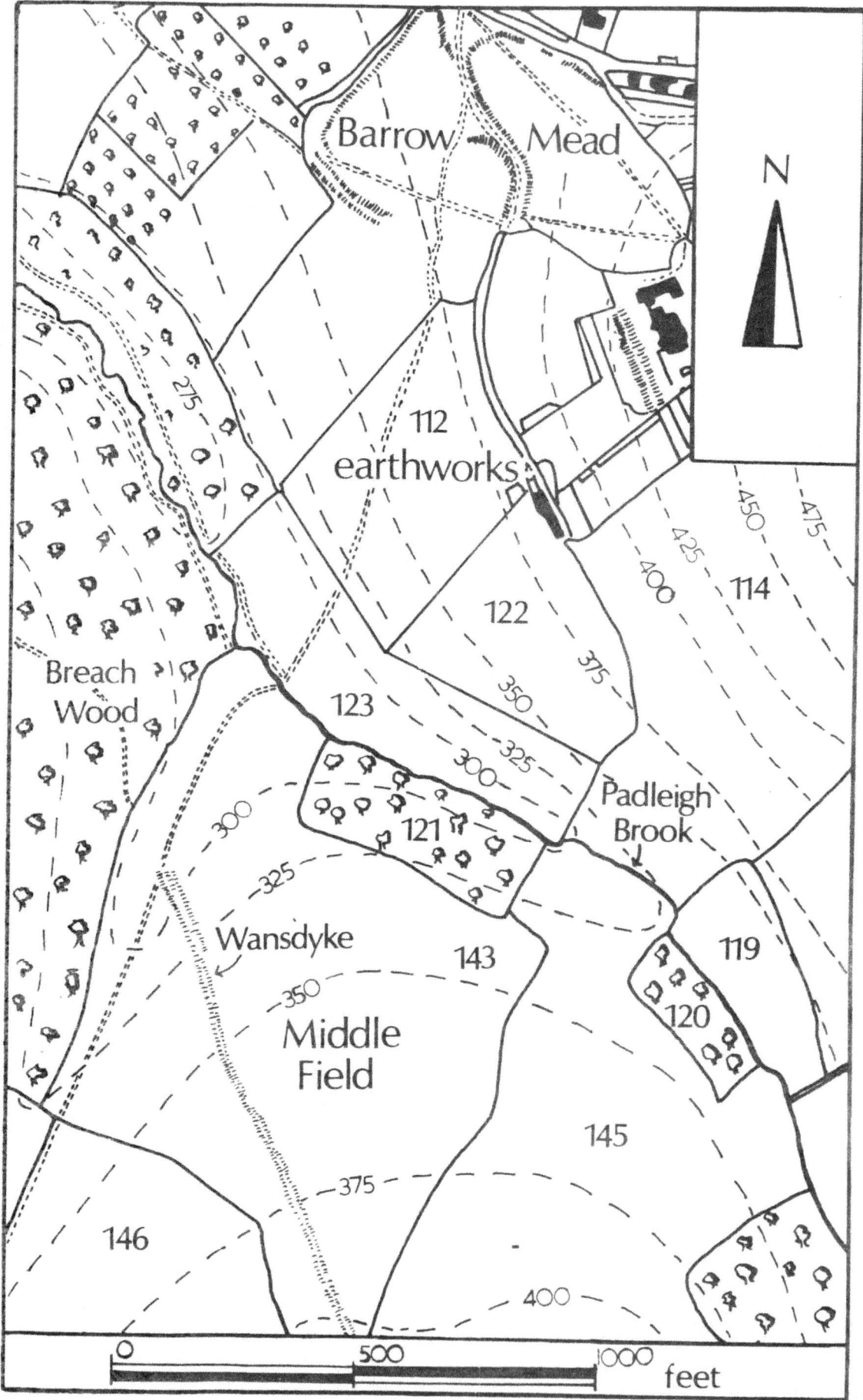

FIG. 1.   Medieval Earthworks near Englishcombe, Somerset, 1959.
(Reproduced from Rahtz 1960-1, fig. 2.)

The earliest reference to Barrow Mead is in 1231 which records a dispute between Thomas de Stok and Rannulf de Hurle over two parts of one hide of land in "Ingelscumbe (Englishcombe) et Berghe" (C.C.R., 1231, 562). In 1315-16 the Nomina Villarum states that Matilda de Baiuse holds "Twyverton (Twerton) cum hameleto de Bergh" (K. Quest, 62). In the same year Twerton, and presumably Bergh, passed into the hands of the Rodney family (C.I.P.M., 1315, 339).

The next reference is in 1442-3 when Henry Champeneys, a local land-owner who served as an escheator in Somerset and Dorset (C.F.R., 16, 174) acquired from John Cleye "four messuages, one hundred and twenty acres of land, twenty four acres of meadow, twenty acres of pasture, six acres of wood, and pasture for two hundred sheep in Neuton Seintlowe (Newton St. Loe), Twyverton, and Barogh juxta Ingelscombe (F.F., 22, 105). In 1452-3 Richard Chokke, who later became a knight, acquired from John Brydde "two messu-ages, two tofts, one hundred and thirty acres of land, ten acres of meadow, thirty acres of pasture, and ten acres of wood in Twyverton, Ingelscombe, and Berewe juxta Bath" (F.F., 22, 115).

There is some documentary evidence for the post-medieval occupation observed in the west of the site. This may be the "Barrow House" recorded on a map of 1742 "Five Miles around Bath" (Rahtz, 1960-1, 70).

DISCUSSION

Bergh is associated with Englishcombe in 1231 and Twerton in 1316. This might imply either that there were two settlements at Barrow Mead, or that one settlement was divided between two manorial holdings. Alternatively, a single settlement may have been transferred from one estate to another. The lands of the Baiuse family were split by inheritance in the 13th century (F. Aids, 1284-5, 279; C.I.P.M., 1296, 249), and this or some earlier divided inheritance might explain a division of Barrow Mead into two.

The references of 1442-3 and 1452-3 to "Barogh juxta Inglescumb" and "Berewe juxta Bath" respectively again raise the possibility of the existence of two settlements at Barrow Mead. There is no indication as to where a division lay, but the general topography of the area (Fig. 1) suggests that Padleigh Brook was the most likely boundary between the two settlements. The earthworks in Middle Field may therefore be the site of Barogh juxta Inglescumb, while Berewe juxta Bath may have comprised the earthworks investigated at Barrow Mead and those in field 112. Barrow Mead is now just inside the parish of Englishcombe, but it is named as part of Twerton in the 1841 Tithe map. It is possible that Padleigh Brook was also the original line of the parish boundary which later moved to the north of the site along the line of the present road (Fig. 1).

CONCLUSIONS

The documentary evidence shows that Barrow Mead was in existence as a hamlet ("cum hamleto de Bergh;" 1315-16; Nomina Villarum) at least from the 14th century. It may of course have originated at a much earlier date, but would escape mention in documents because of its character as a subsidiary settlement. There may have been two separate but adjacent hamlets on each side of Padleigh Brook. The two Barrow names appear in mid-15th century documents, but in both cases they are linked with other places, so it is not possible to say whether or not the settlement(s) still existed as hamlet(s) at that date.

NB. For documentary references see bibliography p. 62.

THE EXCAVATION

DESCRIPTION OF INDIVIDUAL PERIODS

NB. For details of features see Appendix p. 52.

SUMMARY OF PERIODS AND PHASES

Occupation on the site has been divided into periods I-III. Period I is pre-medieval. Periods II and III are both medieval and dated to the 13th-14th centuries, but are distinguished by the change from timber to stone construction. Further sub-divisions were possible within these main periods.

Period I	pre-medieval	
phase A	Iron Age: ditch F1 and associated pottery	
phase B	Roman: eight sherds and one coin	
Period II	medieval timber buildings	
phase A	recutting of F1	
phase B	construction of first timber building	
phase C	construction of second timber building	
Period III	medieval stone buildings	
phase A	construction of earlier stone house	
phase B	construction of later stone house	
	B1 - the original building	
	B2 - earth floor F50 replaced by clay floor F52	
	B3 - narrowing of entrance	
	B4 - realignment of NW wall south of entrance. Clay floor replaced by mortar floor F54.	

PERIOD I: PRE-MEDIEVAL

PHASE A: IRON AGE (Fig. 2)

The earliest occupation of the site is represented by a ditch F1 in the north of the excavated area. Iron Age pottery was found in the lower levels, and mixed with medieval sherds in the higher levels (Fig. 5, Section CD). There was not enough time to excavate this feature completely, and so sections BC (Fig. 6), CD and DF (Fig. 5) are thus incomplete. F2 and F3 (Fig. 3) may bear some relationship to the ditch: these ambiguous features are discussed below with the timber buildings of period II. Single Iron Age sherds

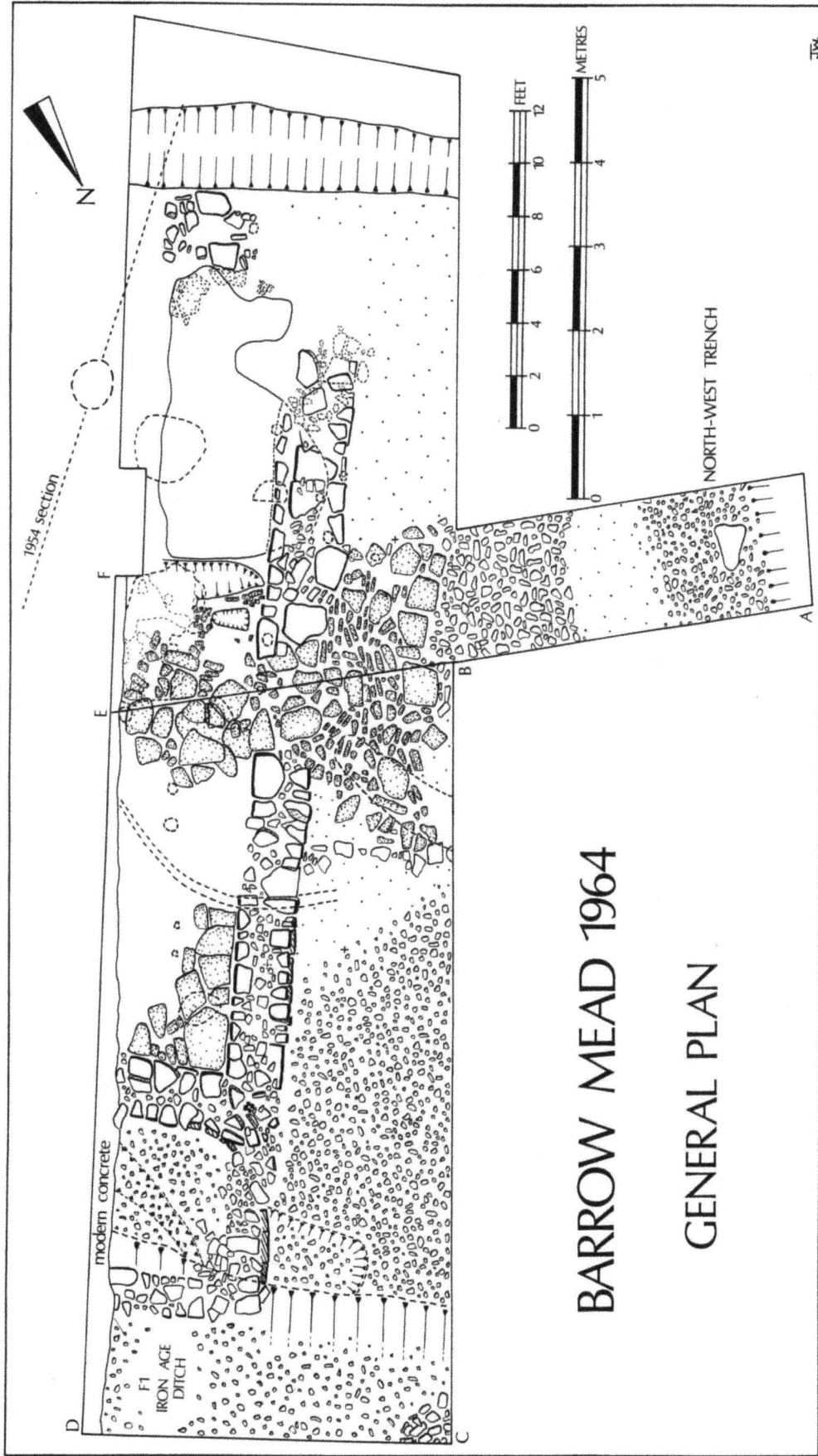

BARROW MEAD 1964

GENERAL PLAN

NORTH-WEST TRENCH

FEET

METRES

1954 section

modern concrete

F1
IRON AGE
DITCH

N

FIG. 2

were found in the metalling F4 (probably as a result of disturbance when this was laid over the ditch in period IIB), and in the topsoil.

PHASE B: ROMAN

Four sherds of Roman coarse pottery were recovered from the ditch F1, stratified between the Iron Age and medieval levels (Fig. 5, Section CD). Three fragments of samian were also found scattered over the site, and a coin of the fourth century was incorporated in the packing of the SW wall F41. No features contained exclusively Roman material.

PERIOD II: TIMBER BUILDINGS (Figs. 2, 3, 6)

Excavations in 1954 failed to recover any evidence of timber structures, except for a single feature revealed in the section. All the evidence for period II comes therefore from the 1964 investigations of the site which defined three successive phases of occupation.

F2 and F3 are very difficult to place within this framework, mostly because their relationship with the Iron Age ditch F1 was not clearly demonstrable during excavation. F2 was originally described as a timber slot, and F3 as a pit, both apparently cut by F1 (as recut in the medieval period), and sealed by the metalling F4 of period IIB. There was no pottery or small finds in either to give any indication of date. Four possible interpretations are suggested:

1. They are earlier than F1, and thus the earliest features on the site.
2. Both features are contemporary with F1, acting as a drain leading into it and an additional soak-away.
3. They belong to the earliest phase of medieval occupation and were truncated when F1 was recut at a later stage. In this case the interpretation of the features as a timber slot and pit would be valid, and an earlier phase of timber building would have to be postulated, possibly of an aceramic period.
4. The features are contemporary with the medieval recut of F1 and have the same function as in 2. The sides of the ditch would in this case have later weathered back and would appear to have cut them.

PHASE A (Fig. 3)

The first positive evidence of medieval occupation on the site is associated with material in the upper part of F1. There is no silting between the Roman and medieval finds, suggesting that the upper part of the ditch was recut (Fig. 5). The presence of Iron Age pottery in the medieval levels is probably due to disturbance during recutting, or to the weathering of the surrounding area.

PHASE B (Fig. 3)

This phase can be separated from the preceding one by the layer of metalling F4 which sealed the recut ditch F1 (Fig. 5, Section CD; Fig. 6, Sections AE, BC), F2 and F3. This metalling was located to the NW and NE of the

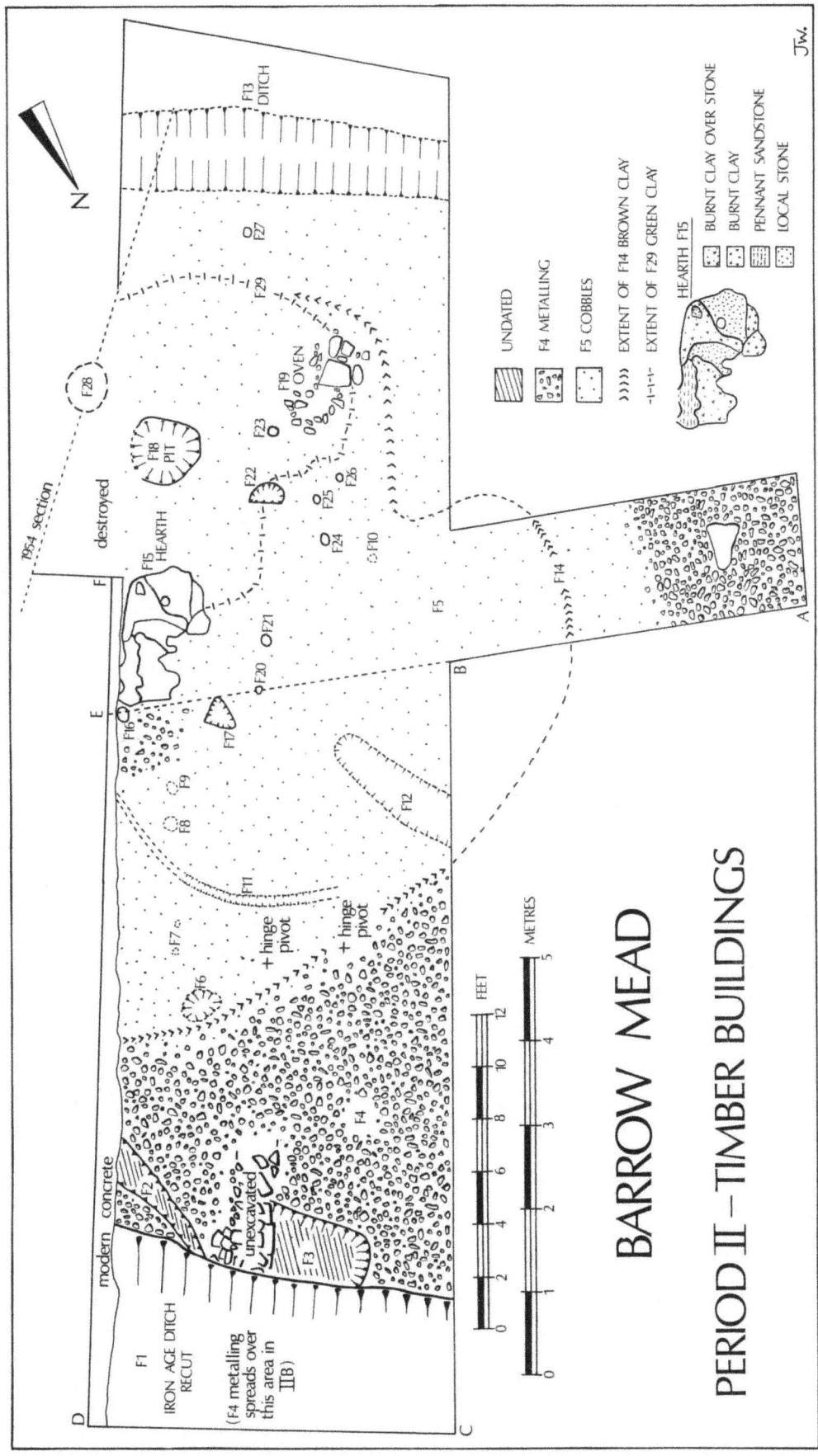

N

F13 DITCH

1954 section

destroyed

F28

F27

F29

F18 PIT

F19 OVEN

F23

F22

F25   F26

F24

F10

F5 HEARTH

F20   F21

F16

F17

F9

F8

F11

F12

F14

F5

F7

F6

+ hinge pivot

+ hinge pivot

F4

F3

F2

F1

modern concrete

IRON AGE DITCH RECUT

(F4 metalling spreads over this area in IIB)

unexcavated

D

E

F

A

B

C

UNDATED
F4 METALLING
F5 COBBLES
EXTENT OF F14 BROWN CLAY
EXTENT OF F29 GREEN CLAY
HEARTH F15
BURNT CLAY OVER STONE
BURNT CLAY
PENNANT SANDSTONE
LOCAL STONE

FEET
0 2 4 6 8 10 12

METRES
0 1 2 3 4 5

Jw.

BARROW MEAD
PERIOD II—TIMBER BUILDINGS

FIG. 3

later stone house where it probably continued in use, to the north of the hearth F15 of phase C, and throughout the North-West Trench. It may have originally covered the area where the earlier stone house was built. A layer of cobbles F5 extended over most of the remaining area, and faded out in the North-West Trench where they overlay the F4 metalling (Fig. 6, Section AE). This may imply that the metalling and the cobbles belong to two separate phases, or more probably that two layers of stones were needed here where the ground sloped away to build up the surface and prevent mud accumulating. The cobbles are interpreted as a floor and the metalling as an area outside the building.

The features of IIB were all cut into the cobbles and were separated from the later phases by a layer of brown clay F14. They consist of post holes F6-F10; and F11 and F12 (Fig. 3). F11 and the post holes around it were filled with the same greyish-brown soil, suggesting they are contemporary. Two hinge pivots (Fig. 11, nos. 18,19) were found at the same level. These may be important in giving some indication of where an entrance was, and suggest that there was a substantial timber door, and not one of wattle and daub or some similar light material. This interpretation must be treated cautiously however, because these fixtures may equally be associated with gates or window shutters (personal communication, Ian H. Goodall). They do indicate a degree of sophistication in the structure of the house if entrances/ gateways were being closed by timber doors or gates. Equally they may represent the only evidence for windows from the site.

Ditch F13 probably belongs to IIB as the cobbles extended right up to it, and the 1954 section (Rahtz, 1960-1, Fig. 5) shows it was backfilled with brown clay similar to that which sealed the other features (F14). This does not preclude the possibility that it may have been dug in IIA and continued in use during phase B.

PHASE C (Fig. 3)

The features of the final timber building are distinguished by being cut into the brown clay layer F14. Some were separated from the later stone house by layer F29.

F15 was a hearth, originally built of local stone, and later resurfaced with clay and pennant sandstone. Two post holes F16 and F17 were thought by the excavator to be associated with the hearth: they may have been part of a superstructure, perhaps a hood or chimney. F19 was a stone oven base with an ashy area to the NE, where a lump of burnt daub was found. This may indicate that the oven was covered by a clay hood. F18 was interpreted by the excavator as a latrine pit: its position between the hearth and oven would in this case be an unusual one. The rest of the features were post holes which may not have been contemporary. A further feature of unknown dimensions and function (F28) was located in the 1954 section sealed by F29. It was initially thought to be a continuation of F18: from its position on the plan this seems unlikely, and it has been indicated as a separate feature.

Layer F29 was found to seal many of the features of phase IIC. The extent of this layer was not planned, but has been approximately plotted in

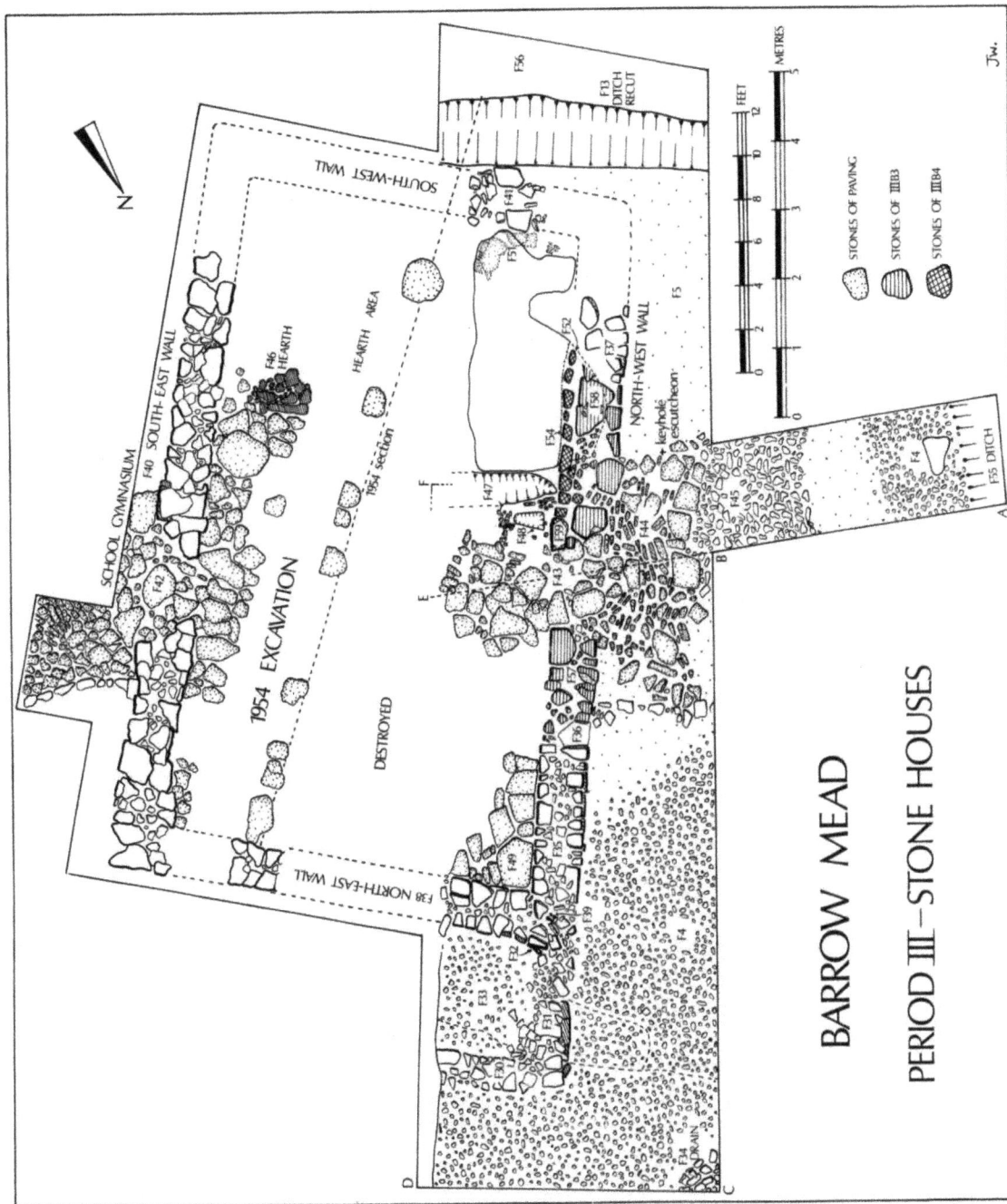

BARROW MEAD

PERIOD III – STONE HOUSES

FIG. 4

Fig. 3 from observations in the records. It is described by the excavator as two layers of green clay separated by a thin charcoal layer, and it appears in the 1954 section (Rahtz, 1960-1, Fig. 5) as layer 5 "laminated charcoal and yellow clay". This may be the destruction layer of wattle and daub walls which have been partly burnt and have collapsed inwards, or the remains of a canopy over the hearth and oven.

PERIOD III: STONE HOUSES (Figs. 2, 4, 7; Pl. 4)

PHASE A (Fig. 4)

The first stone house is represented by the remains of three walls, F30, F31 and F32 in the north of the excavated area. The bottom courses of F32 could be seen below the line of the NE wall of the later stone house. The east part of the building had been destroyed by the school, but it is assumed that it was orientated east-west. If that is correct, the building was 9 ft 6 ins wide externally, 5 ft 6 ins internally, and of unknown length. Traces of a floor F33 were found - this is probably the same layer as the metalling F4 which was thought to cover this area. Outside the house, the metalling F4 and cobbles F5 may have remained in use as a yard.

F34 is interpreted as a drain, cutting through F4 metalling (Fig. 5, section CD; Fig. 6, section BC). It may be associated with the later stone house, but is perhaps too far away to belong to this phase.

PHASE B (Fig. 4)

General

In period IIIB the main stone house on the site was erected. The remains of all four walls survived to heights of between two and five courses, with opposing entrances in the middle of each long side. Associated features within the house and outside it were also recovered. The building was orientated NE-SW, and its approximate dimensions were 34 x 21 ft externally, 30 x 17 ft internally at the north end; the south end was 1 ft narrower. The walls were packed with clay which appears to have been scraped up from the immediate area. This disturbance is probably an important reason why no more timber features of period II were recovered.

General remarks will first be made about construction techniques and materials used in the walls, entrances, floors, and associated features inside and outside the building. This is followed by descriptions of individual phases IIIB1-IIIB4. IIIB1 represents the original building, and IIIB2-4 later modifications to it.

Construction techniques and materials: associated features (Fig. 4)

The walls of the house were all composed of well dressed masonry packed with clay. F35, the NW wall to the north of the entrance lay in a shallow foundation trench packed with brown clayey soil which cut through F4 metalling. F37 is the continuation of this wall to the south of the entrance. Part of the NE wall F38 uncovered in 1964 appears to have used the footings of the

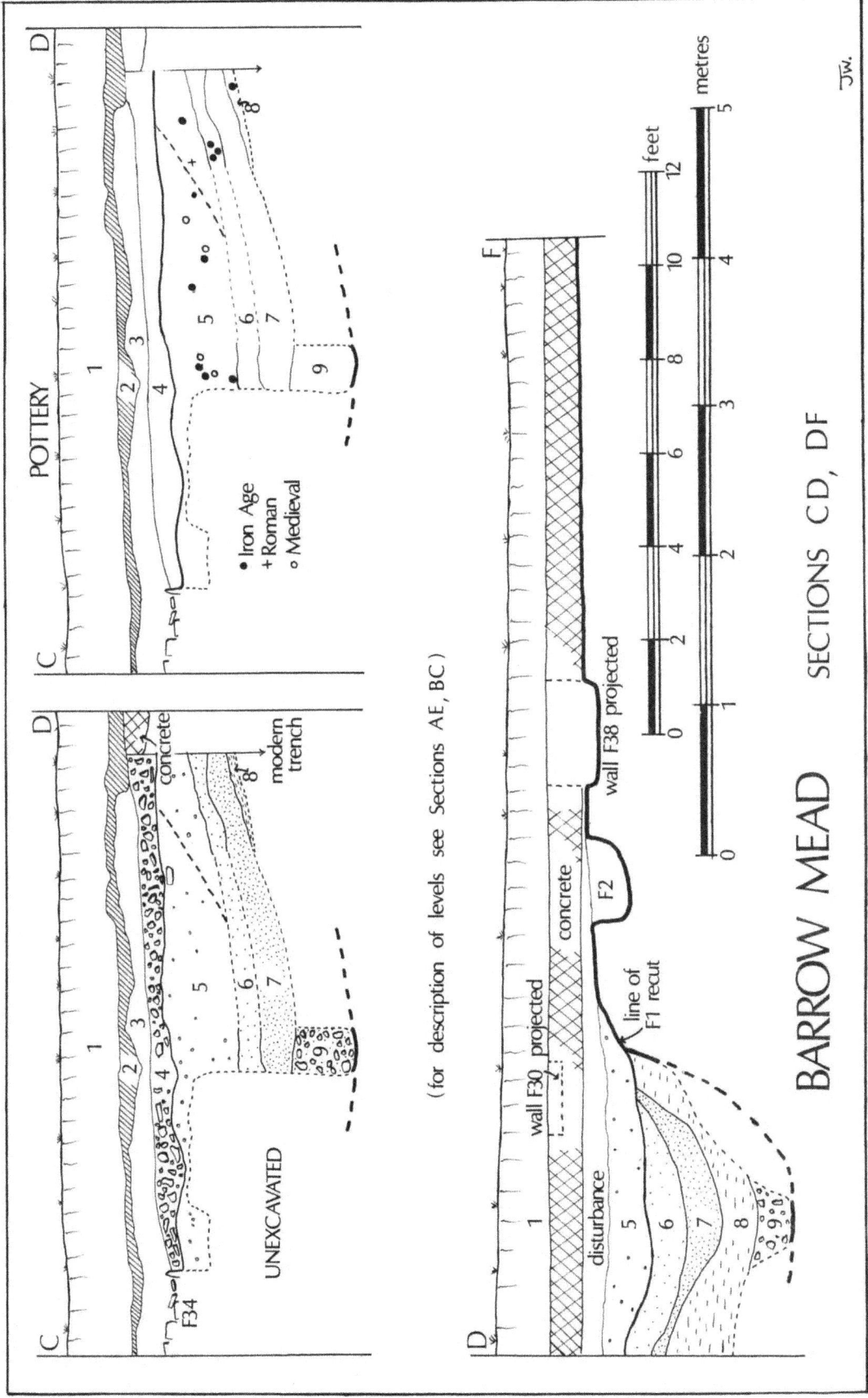

POTTERY

- Iron Age
+ Roman
o Medieval

UNEXCAVATED

concrete

modern trench

F34

(for description of levels see Sections AE, BC)

wall F30 projected

disturbance

concrete

F2

line of F1 recut

wall F38 projected

feet

metres

BARROW MEAD   SECTIONS CD, DF

FIG. 5

JW.

IIIA stone house as a foundation. The 1954 section also cut through this wall: here it appeared to be set in a construction trench filled with charcoal flecked brown soil (Rahtz, 1960-1, Fig. 5, layer 2). At the junction of F35 and F38 a small post hole F39 was recovered, which probably held a corner post. Only a few stones of the SW wall F41 were seen, which were difficult to distinguish from the spread of rubble in this area. The SE wall F40 was excavated in 1954. It had been laid directly on the original ground surface (Rahtz, 1960-1, 66).

The positions of two entrances were located: F42 in the SE wall was 2 ft 6 ins wide, splaying outwards to 5 ft 6 ins, and opened onto a carefully laid paved yard bounded on one side by a low wall (Rahtz, 1960-1, 68). The NW entrance F43 originally extended from F35 to F37, making it 15 ft 9 ins wide, but was later narrowed. It was made up of large flat stones, very worn, packed with brown clayey earth, and lay on brown soil. It opened onto a similar paved yard F44 with boundary wall. In the North-West Trench the yard continued as a layer of metalling F45, and then as the metalling F4 and cobbles F5. F4 and F5 probably continued in use outside the house where they do not seem to be covered by any later layers.

Associated features inside the house include F47, interpreted as a timber slot for a wooden partition, and F48 a post hole associated with it. These features would seem to have been in use during the whole of period IIIB as they were not sealed by any later layers, and the floor levels ran up to F47.

The division of the interior was reflected in the character of the floor surface. To the north of the partition the floor was composed of stone slabs F49 which were replaced at intervals. To the south of the partition the floor surface changed frequently throughout period IIIB.

A hearth F46 was excavated in 1954. This appears to have been used throughout IIIB as there are signs that it was periodically resurfaced. Traces of ash from here were seen in the 1954 section.

At the same time as the house was built, ditch F13 was recut up to a depth of 1 ft, probably for drainage. The upcast may have been used to raise the floor level in phase IIIB2. The relationship of the levels F56 outside the ditch to period IIIB cannot be determined.

A further feature F55 in the North-West Trench may be associated with this period. This was interpreted as a ditch by the excavator, but was incompletely excavated and so is difficult to place within the sequence.

PHASE IIIB1

During this phase the entrance extended from F35 to F37. It is likely that the whole of the entrance was originally paved, but that some slabs were removed when F57 and F58 were built.

To the south of the partition F47, the floor was composed of a mixed ashy soil F50, with straw impressions on the surface, and the remains of eggshells, cockles and mussels. The extent of this was not plotted on the plan, but it is believed to have been similar to that of F52. A few floor slabs F51 near the SW wall belong to this phase.

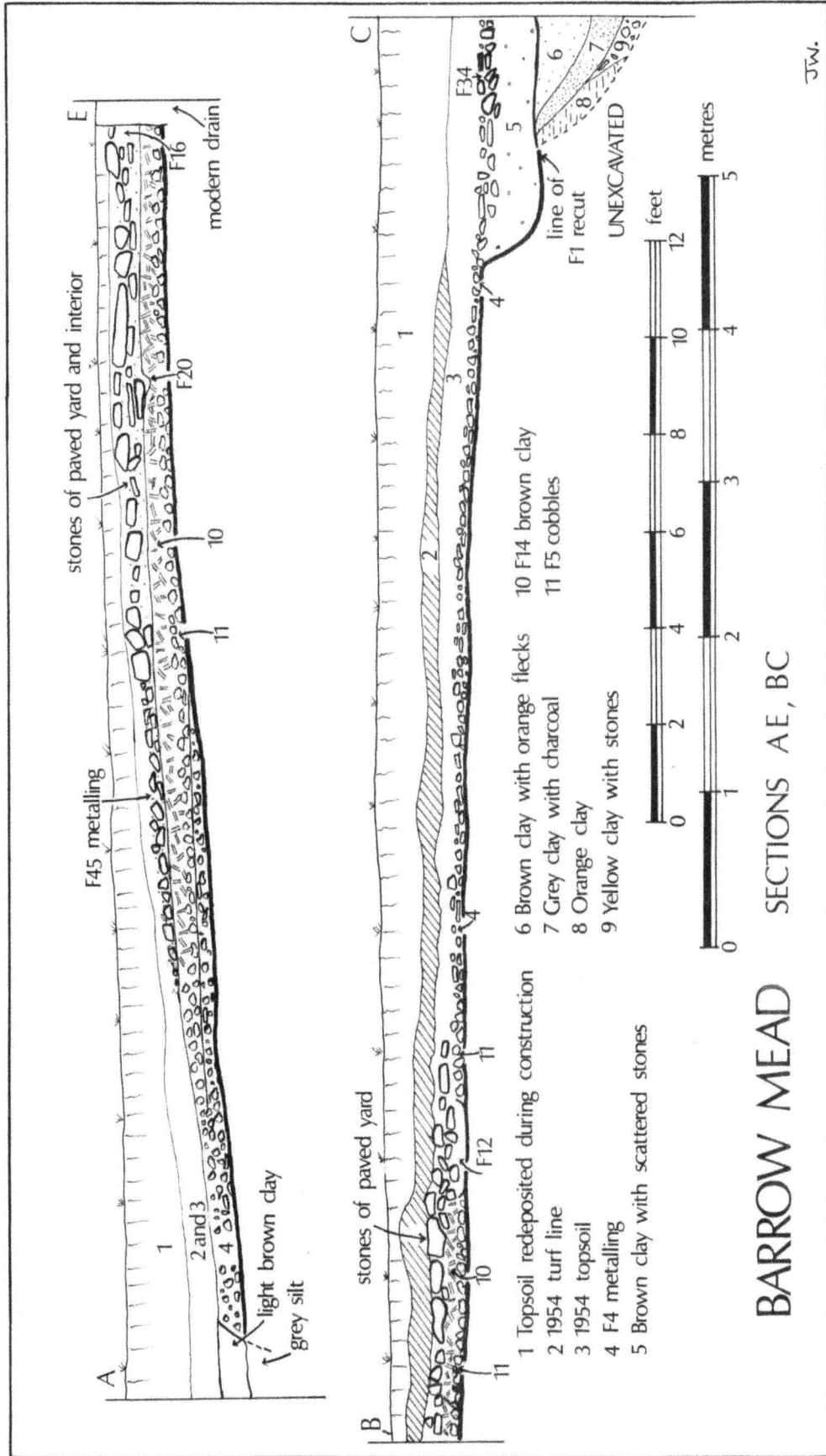

Section A–E:

- stones of paved yard and interior
- modern drain
- F16
- F20
- F45 metalling
- 10
- 11
- 2 and 3
- 4
- light brown clay
- grey silt
- 1

Section B–C:

- stones of paved yard
- F34
- F12
- line of F1 recut
- UNEXCAVATED
- 5
- 6
- 7
- 8
- 9
- 10
- 11
- 4
- 3
- 2
- 1

Legend:

1 Topsoil redeposited during construction
2 1954 turf line
3 1954 topsoil
4 F4 metalling
5 Brown clay with scattered stones
6 Brown clay with orange flecks
7 Grey clay with charcoal
8 Orange clay
9 Yellow clay with stones
10 F14 brown clay
11 F5 cobbles

feet
0 2 4 6 8 10 12

metres
0 1 2 3 4 5

BARROW MEAD   SECTIONS AE, BC

FIG. 6

JW.

PHASE IIIB2

In this phase a layer of clay and stones F52 was spread over the earth floor F50. This may have been the upcast from the recutting of F13. It may have been slightly more extensive than on the plan, as the 1954 section shows traces of clay flooring (Rahtz, 1960-1, Fig. 5, layer 3). The fact that F52 was extended under F58 and F59 reinforces the idea that as yet there was no wall in this area. Three spindle-whorls and a hone are associated with this floor. (Fig. 11, nos. 1, 3-5).

A green cessy concretion F53 (not indicated on the plan) covered F52 and was mixed up with it. It was interpreted by the excavator as a layer of human cess which had accumulated on the clay floor and probably drained outwards through the open wall.

PHASE IIIB3

The alterations of this phase resulted in the narrowing of the NW entrance F43 to 4 ft (Pl. 3). To achieve this, the line of F35 was continued by a further length of wall F57. The later masonry could be distinguished because it lay on a layer of black soil, instead of a bottom course of stones like F35. F36 was a gap in the wall at the junction of F57 and F35. It was filled with black earth below which was a single flat stone. It is suggested that F36 belongs to phase IIIB3 from the evidence of a sketch section (not illustrated) which shows it to lie on the same black soil that continues under F57. This is possibly where a timber stud was placed.

A further length of the NW wall F58 was built northwards from F37. The stones here sit on a 5 ins layer of brown clay and gravel. This addition may not have taken place at the same time as F57 was built, but there is no evidence to separate the two alterations chronologically.

PHASE IIIB4

During this phase the alignment of the NW wall to the south of the entrance was improved by building a further row of stones F59 on the inside.

The floor surface was raised again, this time using mortar F54. It extended up to the realigned stone wall, and then followed the line of F52. There was a small amount of disturbance through the floor levels F54-F52.

The keyhole escutcheon found in the topsoil (Fig. 11, no. 20) may possibly belong to phases IIIB3 or 4. This, together with a key recovered in 1954 (Rahtz, 1960-1, fig. 8, no. 4) points to substantial wooden doors.

It is suggested that little or no time elapsed between the alterations of phases IIIB3 and 4.

DATING: PERIODS II AND III

The dating of periods II and III is based solely on the evidence of the pottery and two coins. Medieval pottery can rarely be closely dated as coarse fabrics and forms were current over long periods. Site dating is usually based on associations with imported pottery, or external parallels from better dated contexts.

Two sherds only (Fabric F) may on general grounds be pre-1100. They occur in F1 and F18, but in both contexts are with pottery of a later date. This makes a pre-Conquest date for the early occupation of the site unlikely.

The bulk of the pottery falls within the 13th-14th centuries. It is not possible to date the individual phases within the complex on the basis of the pottery. There is no demonstrable development in pottery style between periods II and III, nor any difference in the proportion of type-fabrics. It can only be said that the medieval occupation at Barrow Mead did not last long enough for any major changes in pottery style to take place.

The dating of the site can be narrowed on the evidence of two coins:

1. A coin issued c. 1258-72 found in 1954 (Rahtz, 1960-a, 68) suggests a late 13th century or later date for the use of the yard where it was found.
2. A jetton c. 1370-1400 (Rahtz, 1960-1, 69) suggests a late 14th century or later date for the use of the hearth (F46) which cannot be tied to a particular structural phase.

If none of the pottery from the site is later than 1400, the use of at least one feature within the buildings can be tied to the later years of the 14th century.

From the evidence available it can be suggested that the main occupation of the site spanned the 14th century and that desertion probably took place c. 1400.

DISCUSSION

PERIOD I

Iron Age pottery was recovered during the excavation from the ditch F1. The sherds are of Glastonbury type, which is assigned to the South-Western B cultures (Hawkes, 1959). Barrow Mead lies along the NE edge of its distribution (Peacock, 1969, Fig. 1). The Barrow Mead sherds have not yet been submitted to Peacock for examination, so it is not possible to say which group they belong to. The pottery has not been discussed in detail, and reference should be made to a forthcoming specialist report (A. Ellison, thesis in preparation; personal communication).

Several ditches and pits containing similar pottery were located in 1954 among the earthworks (Rahtz, 1960-1, 70): sufficient to suggest an occupation site. Just above the site is a prominent spur which may have been adapted to a hillfort: there are traces of scarping on the slope (Rahtz, 1960-1, 71), now largely obliterated by modern landscaping, and some dry stone revetment along the south side of the spur. If these 'defences' are Iron Age, the features excavated at Barrow Mead are of interest because they represent the remains of an extra-mural settlement, such as site B at Cannington (Rahtz, 1969a, 60). Unfortunately the nature of the settlement cannot be assessed on the basis of so little evidence.

The Roman material however was confined to a few sherds stratified in F1, some fragments of samian and a coin. The number of finds was so small that it is unlikely to represent any significant occupation of the site. There is a Roman villa only two miles north of Barrow Mead at Newton St. Loe (marked on the One Inch O.S. map, sheet no. 166). It is possible that the material found at Barrow Mead was loosely associated with its sphere of influence.

PERIOD II (Fig. 3)

PHASE A

The recut ditch F1 is the only definite feature that can be associated with the earliest medieval occupation of the site. Other features may have been destroyed by later disturbance, or may lie beyond the limits of the 1964 excavation.

PHASE B

There are comparatively more features associated with phase B, but their interpretation is difficult. It was suggested by the excavator that F11 was an eaves-drip runnell and therefore indicated the line of one of the walls. It seems more likely that this was a drain, leading to a sump F12. Of the post holes, only F5 seems substantial enough to have supported a major structural timber; the rest are mere depressions in the ground and perhaps represent internal features such as partitions. Ditch F13 may have been for drainage.

PHASE C

At the end of phase B, much of the area was covered with a layer of brown clayey soil with some stones (F14; Fig. 6, Section AE). This may have been a deliberate building up of the surface using redeposited natural clay. However it covers an area roughly corresponding with that of the cobbles F5, (Fig. 3) and so may represent the destruction level of a timber building whose super-structure was largely of wattle and daub or clay wall construction.

The extent of the cobbles F5, metalling F4 and brown clay F14 gives some indication of the area covered by the building. It implies that quite an extensive structure had been erected on the site, whose character cannot now be determined.

The green clay F29 which sealed many of the features of phase C could also be interpreted as a destruction layer. If this is correct, then it may give some indication of the dimensions of the final timber building. It suggests that an oven was built into one of the walls, and a hearth was situated near the outside (Fig. 3). A chimney or hood as previously suggested (p.10) would reduce the possibilities of a fire risk. Alternatively the extent of F29 may not represent the limits of the house: a similar clay was used for packing the SW wall of the later stone house, suggesting that much of layer F29 had been removed for this purpose. The building erected in phase C may have therefore covered a larger area than the remaining evidence suggests.

During phase C it appears that a substantial timber dwelling house was constructed with a heart and oven. The fact that the hearth had been resurfaced and layers F14 and F5 below it had been burnt through suggests that this phase was not of a very short duration.

CONCLUSIONS (Period II)

At least three phases of medieval timber building are represented on the site, and the use of wattle and daub in construction is suggested by the material of phases B and C. Unfortunately not enough features have survived to reconstruct the entire plans of the buildings nor to make any definite conclusions about their character and function. Clearly excavation has revealed only a fraction of the evidence for occupation during period II. It is suggested that during the construction of the later stone house clay was scraped up from the immediate area for wall packing (see p. 12). This disturbance is likely to have been responsible for the destruction of many of the features of period II.

PERIOD III (Fig. 4)

PHASE A

The first stone house is built on an area already much disturbed by earlier occupation F1, F2 and F3. In spite of this the only measure taken to counteract the effects of an unstable subsoil was to insert a large foundation for the NW wall F31 into the silt of F3. This might imply that there was a time of lapse between periods IIC and IIIA in which the extensive disturbance was forgotten. Timber structures IIB and C both avoided this area. Sinking may have been a factor in the decision to abandon this house.

The narrowness of building IIIA and the absence of any internal features including a hearth, prompts some discussion as to its function. This may not have been a dwelling at all, but an outhouse associated with some other building. So little of the early stone house was uncovered in 1964 that it is possible that many important features lay outside the excavated area. It is difficult to reach any conclusions about the character and function of the building with so little evidence.

PHASE B: INTERPRETATION (Fig. 7)

General

During period IIIB a good quality stone house was built on the site. It was not laid out to a regular plan, as the SW end was 1 ft shorter than the NW and the walls were not at right angles. It cannot be determined how far the walls were carried up in stone - they may have been only footings for a timber and/or clay superstructure. The width of the walls does however argue against this - the stone may have been extensively robbed, perhaps for use in the 17th-18th century houses elsewhere on the site.

There is no evidence on which to base a reconstruction of the roof: no internal supports were recovered, but evidence for these may have been

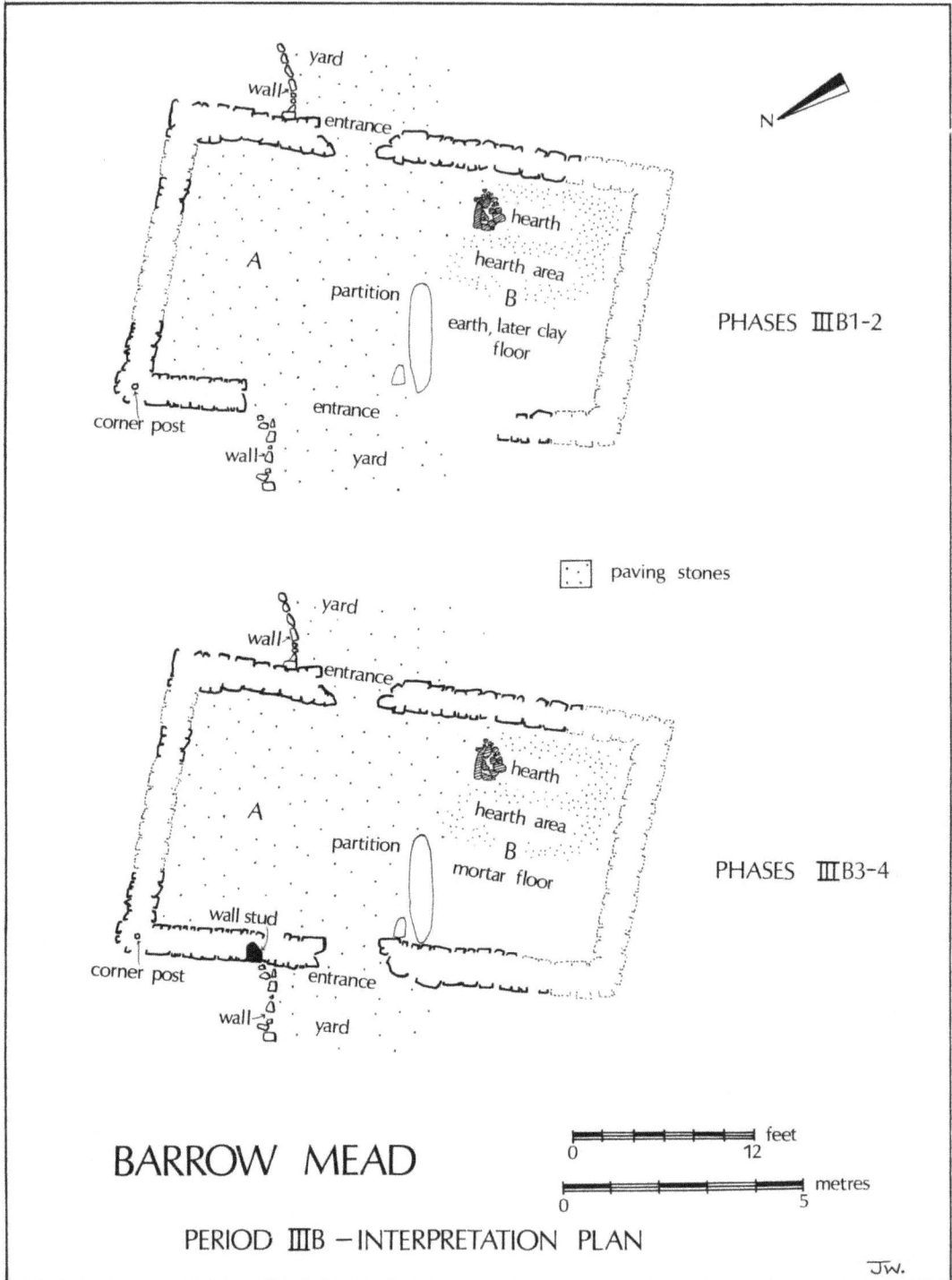

yard

wall

entrance

hearth

hearth area

N

A

partition

B

earth, later clay
floor

PHASES ⅢB1-2

corner post

wall

entrance

yard

☐ paving stones

yard

wall

entrance

hearth

hearth area

A

partition

B

mortar floor

PHASES ⅢB3-4

wall stud

corner post

entrance

wall

yard

BARROW MEAD

feet
0   12

metres
0   5

PERIOD ⅢB — INTERPRETATION PLAN

JW.

FIG. 7

destroyed in the period between the 1954 and 1964 excavations. No roof tiles were found, suggesting the use of thatch, shingles, turf or some similar material.

It is unfortunate that the entire house could not have been excavated at the same time, and that some of the interior and most of the SW wall were lost. Notably absent is any trace of an oven, although this may have been built into the missing wall.

PHASE IIIB1 AND IIIB2 (Fig. 7)

During phases IIIB1 and 2 the plan is reconstructed of a stone house with one wide and one narrow entrance in the middle of each long side which lead onto paved yards bounded by a low wall. Inside the building is shown divided into two rooms, A and B, by a wooden partition inside the NW entrance. The hearth is indicated in room B, and the heavy stippling denotes a spread of ash from here which probably extended as far as the SW wall. The timber partition has been extended up to the hearth area. Floor slabs revealed during excavation are shown covering all of room A. Room B has an earth floor replaced by a clay one in IIIB2 which has also been shown extending to the hearth area. The majority of the finds came from room B: spindle whorls from the clay floor show that spinning was one of the activities carried out here.

The width of the NW entrance and the division of the interior by different floor materials and a partition suggest that this was a typical long house (as defined below p. 23). The position of the hearth, the straw impressions and food remains, the finds and layer of cess all point to the function of room B as a living area. Room A is therefore interpreted as the byre, working area, or store.

Pl. 4 shows how the house in its earlier phases may have looked. It is illustrated as being built entirely of stone with a thatched roof. The wide entrance, internal partition, and the paving and metalling of the exterior are also visible. The masonry appears rather more regular than the excavated walls suggested.

Many of the features shown in Pl. 4 can only be inferred from the evidence, and this emphasises the difficulties of reconstructing a house from the ground plan only. The height of the walls, for instance, is not known, nor the exact material used for roofing. The shape and position of the windows is purely hypothetical. Three dimensional reconstructions are useful in trying to convey the character of the entire building. They should however be regarded in the light of the limitations of the evidence on which they are based.

PHASE IIIB3 and IIIB4 (Fig. 7)

The plan of the final phases of occupation shows the NW entrance narrowed, and a timber stud inserted approximately one third of the way along the NW wall. The NW wall to the south of the entrance is shown realigned, and the extent of the mortar floor which replaced the clay one in room B is indicated. The hearth and partition remain in use.

These alterations would suggest that the function of the building has changed from a longhouse to a farmhouse (as defined below, p. 24). The NW entrance is now too narrow to allow easy access for animals, stores or equipment into room B. This may indicate the erection of a separate farm building or buildings outside the excavated area.

COMMENTS

The page numbers in this discussion all refer to the chapter by Hurst in Beresford and Hurst, 1971. This synthesis of excavations enables many conclusions to be drawn about medieval peasant buildings, and makes it possible to see the excavations at Barrow Mead in a wider context. These however are based largely on the results of excavations of single house sites, such as Barrow Mead. As yet there has been no total excavation of a medieval village: even twenty seasons work at Wharram Percy have only scratched the surface of the evidence there.

Most excavations of late medieval houses have revealed a complex picture of continual rebuilding on the same site, though not necessarily on the same alignment. Stone houses, as at Barrow Mead, were often preceded by timber ones, but subsequent building has usually destroyed all but a few indeterminate features (p. 93). This means that reconstruction of timber house plans is very difficult, if not impossible, and no conclusions can yet be drawn about regional styles of construction.

During the late 12th-early 13th century a change from timber to stone construction occurred in many areas, first in the SW and then in other areas where the materials were available (p. 93). This implies that the change at Barrow Mead was later than usual. The reasons for this are not fully understood: there may have been a lack of timber following extensive forest clearance, or possible social and economic factors at present obscure were responsible (p. 93).

The stones used were always near at hand to preclude the cost and difficulties of transport, and were usually laid directly on the ground. Foundation trenches such as those dug for the NW wall at Barrow Mead are rare, but occur also at Upton (Rahtz, 1969, 8). Clay was the common wall packing, lime mortar being restricted to manorial or ecclesiastical structures.

The question as to how high the walls were carried up in stone is a difficult one. Hurst (p. 94) suggests that if the width is 2-3 ft the walls went to their full height in stone. Footings for a timber structure tend to be narrower (1 ft-1 ft 6 ins) and are often only two courses high. The walls at Barrow Mead were approximately 2 ft wide and stood to a maximum height of five courses, suggesting that these are the remains of a house built entirely of stone.

Houses were built to a great variety of shape and size, and as at Barrow Mead, not always carefully laid out with parallel walls at right angles. The amount of timber available for roofing may have been the determining factor in the size of the house (p. 114).

The reconstruction of the roof may be difficult to determine from remains at ground level. A house c. 18 ft (6 m) wide is the limit for an unsupported roof (p. 115). The house at Barrow Mead falls within this limit, but traces of a central row of supports may have been destroyed with part of the interior. Peasant houses were probably roofed with flimsy branches covered with thatch or turf (p. 99). The decaying roof was one possible reason for the continued rebuilding of the house (p. 99).

Within the building traces of partitions are often recovered and the remains of a central hearth - at Barrow Mead built of stones. The area of charcoal spreading from this may have been for storing ashes and baking (p. 98). Ovens were built into the corner of the room but are rarely found. If one existed at Barrow Mead it presumably lay in the area of the destroyed SW wall.

A variety of materials were used for flooring - stone slabs, earth with straw, clay and mortar are all represented at Barrow Mead. The different composition of the floor surface may give some indication of the function of individual rooms.

Very little information is available on the furniture used inside medieval peasant houses. Usually all that the archaeologist recovers are the remains of metal fittings such as the iron hasp, probably from a chest, recovered in the 1954 excavations (Rahtz, 1960-1, Fig. 8, no. 1).

Hinge pivots (Fig. 11, nos. 18, 19), a keyhole escutcheon (Fig. 11, no. 20) and a key (Rahtz, 1960-1, Fig. 8, no. 4) show that the stone buildings - and possibly the timber ones - at Barrow Mead were closed with substantial wooden doors, and not flimsy structures of wattle and daub or some similar material.

Many stone houses were surrounded by drainage ditches, the upcast from which was used to raise the level of the toft or croft (p. 117). Ditches F13 and F55 may have been dug for this purpose: there is some indication that when F13 was recut in period IIIB the upcast may have been deposited on the old floor surface inside the house, raising it by 3 ins.

The plan of the house in the first two phases of period IIIB has been described as a long house (see above p. 21). This is defined as a building with the living part and various farming activities under the same roof (p. 112). Long houses have been found over large areas where they apparently emerge fully developed in the late 12th - early 13th century. It would be interesting to see if the traces of timber buildings recovered under long houses as at Barrow Mead represent earlier and simpler forms of these structures.

Long houses have a wide variety of size and plan. Excavated examples in Somerset include tripartite long houses at Bineham and Moreton. The former was 66 x 20 ft 6 ins, and partly floored with paving slabs (Dewar, Oct. 1951, 43); the latter was 50 x 20 ft internally (Rahtz, forthcoming, site M98). Neither of these sites have produced sufficient information to provide adequate comparisons with Barrow Mead. At Great Beere in Devon a long house was excavated which was 36 x 16 ft externally and of irregular plan. It was divided internally into three by stone partitions. The hearth was situated in the middle room which is interpreted as the main living area

(Jope and Threlfall, 1958, 118-9). At Hound Tor, Devon, house 1 was 48 x 14 ft internally with opposite entrances in each long side, a central partition, and a hearth in the living area (Minter, 1962-3, 341).

Each of these examples was built of local stone with walls surviving to various heights. The many variations in plan do not make it possible as yet to draw any conclusions about regional styles of construction in the SW of England.

Room B (Fig. 7) of the Barrow Mead house would seem to have been used as a living area. The function of room A is more difficult to determine. Hurst states that a "wide entrance is a good reason for suggesting that it housed cattle" (p. 113). Rahtz however argues that "definite evidence must be found before a byre can be postulated; such as stalls, tethering rings, or substantial manure deposits" (Rahtz, 1969, 96) as wide entrances are capable of alternative explanations. None of these more positive features were found at Barrow Mead, and although the possibility of animals is not excluded, room A could equally have been used as a working area or store.

The change from long house to farm at Barrow Mead has been noted on several other sites. The main living area becomes separated from the byre or barn which are placed in distinct buildings (p. 107). Unfortunately only the dwelling house was recovered at Barrow Mead. The process of change has been observed notably at Upton where the subsidiary buildings were attached to the main dwelling house (Rahtz, 1969, 97), and at Gomeldon where the buildings were arranged round a yard (Algar and Musty, 1969, 91). This however was not a contemporary or universal phenomenon: at Wharram Percy in the 16th century all but one of the buildings were long houses (p. 112). It may reflect the increased prosperity of the owner, an attempt to copy manorial complexes, or perhaps a change in the role of animals.

THE FINDS

The finds from peasant houses can offer some information concerning the economy of the site and the activities carried out there. Numerous finds of a wide variety of materials were recovered from Barrow Mead. Pottery was, as usual, the most common find. Cooking pots with lids, bowls, and jugs were all in use. The very high proportion of glazed ware reinforces the idea that the possession of such pottery was not the prerogative of people high in the social scale (see later p. 40).

Agricultural equipment included scythes, sickles and shears (Fig. 11, nos. 25-27). It is possible that some of the knives (Fig. 11, nos. 13-17) were used for this purpose. The variety of size suggests an equal variety of uses. The hones would have been used for sharpening these tools.

Among the household activities spindle-whorls (Fig. 11, nos. 3-5) provide evidence of spinning, and a thimble (Fig. 11, no. 9) of sewing. Music of some sort was provided by a bone whistle (Fig. 11, no. 11).

Unfortunately no animal bones were recovered during the excavations, though this may be due to the acidity of the soil. As a result little information is available on the economy of the site, or the diet of its occupants. The presence of cockle and mussel shells, and fragments of egg shell show that shellfish and eggs were eaten. Indirect evidence for the keeping of sheep is provided by the shears and spindle-whorls, though whether the wool was more **important than the meat** is unknown. The remains of a horseshoe (Fig. 11, **no. 23) and a spur (Rahtz,** 1960-1, Fig. 8, no. 3) show that the horse was a means of transport.

Objects of a more luxurious nature such as the jet bead (Fig. 11, no. 12) and the fragment of a glass vessel (Fig. 11, no. 10) may indicate that this was a fairly prosperous and well-to-do household.

The finds suggest that trading contacts were not extensive. The pottery is all of local manufacture, and the stone objects were not brought from any great distance. It is more difficult to say where the metal objects came from. Some of the more specialized pieces such as keys and locks may have been made at specialised workshops some distance from the site. On the whole, however, Barrow Mead appears to have been a fairly closed community.

CLIMATIC DETERIORATION

Modifications similar to those that were made to the IIIB stone house – narrowing the entrance and raising the floor levels – have been interpreted on some sites as archaeological evidence for climatic deterioration during the later 13th-early 14th century. At Great Beere it was suggested that the north door was blocked to prevent water washing into the house in wet conditions (Jope and Threlfall, 1958, 120). At Holworth ditch digging and raising the floor level were attributed to increasing rainfall (Rahtz, 1959, 136-7). In the case of Barrow Mead these factors coincide with a change in the function of the building to a dwelling only and can equally be interpreted as an attempt to improve living conditions. There does not seem to be sufficient evidence to associate these changes with climatic deterioration.

DESERTION

Barrow Mead appears to have been deserted some time at the end of the 14th century. A few sherds of 16th-17th century date were recovered from the topsoil, but this is not sufficient evidence to postulate continuing occupation. After a period of abandonment the site was reoccupied in the 17th-18th century when what appears to have been a single house or farm was erected. No reasons for the medieval desertion of Barrow Mead are suggested at this stage.

LIMITATIONS OF THE EXCAVATION

The two excavations at Barrow Mead took place under rescue conditions and were separated by a ten year interval during which time some destruction of the site continued. If the whole of the site had been excavated intact, more features of Iron Age and medieval timber buildings may have been recovered, and the nature and function of the IIIA stone house ascertained. Destruction of the interior of the later stone house may have removed the evidence of possible roof supports, therefore limiting any discussion of the superstructure. As excavations were confined to the area of the IIIB stone house, no information about the toft area is available. The change from long house to dwelling in period IIIB would suggest that at least during the latter phases of occupation there were outbuildings here which have not been recovered.

Another considerable limitation is the fact that our knowledge of the other earthworks on the site is limited to the results of a few trial trenches. The nature of the Iron Age features and their relationship to the later occupation of the site cannot be determined. Also the sequence of medieval buildings established on a single house site must stand in isolation, and not within the general pattern of settlement. It would have been interesting to see whether the changes from timber to stone construction and from long house to farm-house occurred simultaneously over the site, and to compare finds and building plans. Only in this way would it have been possible to build up a picture of the origin-growth-decline of the site, and to make suggestions about the relative prosperity and status of its inhabitants.

The lack of an extensive environmental study is a further shortcoming. With suitable conditions for preservation, seed and charcoal identification and pollen analysis would have added further information on the economy of the site, and built up a picture of the surrounding vegetation.

DESERTED MEDIEVAL VILLAGES IN SOMERSET

In 1974, 58 deserted medieval villages were known in Somerset, of which 4 are unlocated (Contitona, Wiftuna, Dudesham, Millescota). This number contrasts sharply with the 107 identified in Wiltshire, and represents mainly the lack of research in this area. Fig. 8 shows the 54 identified sites, including Barrow Mead. The sites have been plotted from the gazetteer in Beresford and Hurst (1971, 202-3), from reports in Archaeological Review (ed. Fowler, 1966-74), and from personal information from M. Aston. It must be emphasised that there has been no systematic study of D.M.V.s in Somerset, and so this distribution is largely a reflection of the areas in which fieldwork has been carried out. As a result the conclusions which are drawn at this stage are only tentative and are likely to be considerably modified by future research.

Some significant factors do however emerge from Fig. 8. The Somerset D.M.V.s known at present fall broadly into two distinct topographical groups. The first group lie on, or at the fringe of, high ground: in the north and NE of the county, on the Blackdown Hills, and around the Quantocks. The second group are on lower ground, in the valley of the Parrett and its tributaries.

The group of sites in the NE include Barrow Mead, and their distribution has been studied in greater detail for this reason. They have been plotted onto a simplified geological map of the area (Fig. 9) which shows the majority to be on clay soils, which might be considered marginal for arable cultivation.

The area was one of the more densely settled in the county at the time of Domesday (Darby, 1967, Fig. 39). There was however still some woodland (of the underwood variety) remaining to be cleared (Darby, 1967, Fig. 41). The area was more heavily stocked with sheep than the rest of Somerset (Darby, 1967, 208).

FIG. 8

D.M.V.s. IN SOMERSET

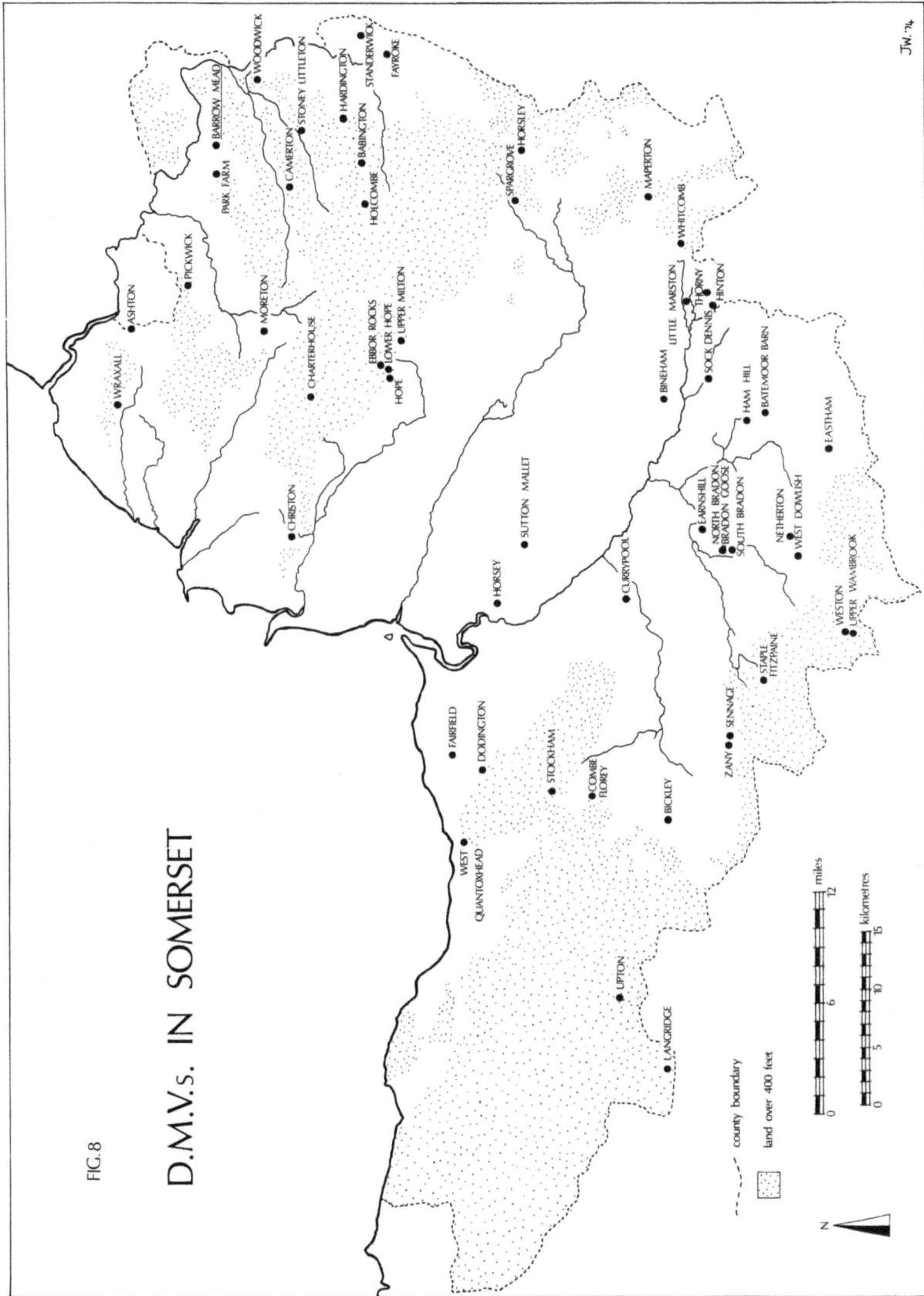

JW. '74

Legend:
- - - county boundary
- land over 400 feet

N

miles
0   6   12

kilometres
0   5   10   15

Place names:

WOODWICK
BARROW MEAD
STONEY LITTLETON
HARDINGTON
STANDERWICK
FAYROKE
PARK FARM
CAMERTON
BABINGTON
HOLCOMBE
HORSLEY
SPARGROVE
PICKWICK
ASHTON
WRAXALL
MORETON
CHARTERHOUSE
FIBBOR ROCKS
LOWER HOPE
UPPER MILTON
HOPE
MAPERTON
WHITCOMB
LITTLE MARSTON
THORNY
HINTON
SOCK DENNIS
BINEHAM
HAM HILL
BATEMOOR BARN
EASTHAM
CHRISTON
SUTTON MALLET
EARNSHILL
NORTH BRADON
BRADON GOOSE
SOUTH BRADON
NETHERTON
WEST DOWLISH
HORSEY
CURRYPOOL
WESTON
UPPER WAMBROOK
STAPLE FITZPAINE
FAIRFIELD
DODINGTON
STOCKHAM
COMBE FLOREY
BICKLEY
ZANY
SENNICK
WEST QUANTOXHEAD
UPTON
LANGRIDGE

The group of sites in the south are generally low-lying, in an area where the subsoil is predominantly clay. The river valleys seem to have contained a below average population in 1086 (Darby, 1967, 182). A considerable amount of woodland remained to be cleared in this area (Darby, 1967, Fig. 41).

Many of the Somerset D.M.V.s are hamlets similar in size to Barrow Mead (personal communication, Mr. P. A. Rahtz), rather than large nucleated villages. Size of the settlement may, as Beresford suggests (Beresford and Hurst, 1971, 20), have been an important factor in their desertion.

The two major areas largely devoid of D.M.V.s are:

1. the marshy lowlands between the rivers Parrett and Axe; much of which is now reclaimed; and

2. the high ground rising towards Exmoor in the west.

Beresford suggests that in Lincolnshire marshy areas reclaimed in medieval times were not particularly vulnerable to desertion (Beresford and Hurst, 1971, 30), and this may be relevant to Somerset also. On the higher ground of the Exmoor fringe, the nucleated village may not have been the predominant unit of settlement, and the area was markedly less densely populated than the rest of the county in 1086 (Darby, 1967, Fig. 39).

The D.M.V.s of Wiltshire provide a comparison for the Somerset distribution (Fig. 10). Again they fall roughly into two area-groupings:

1. the clay vale in the north and NW of the county; the area drained by the Bristol Avon and upper Thames;

2. along the river valleys of Salisbury Plain.

Both areas were well populated in 1086 (Darby, 1967, Fig. 7).

To conclude, therefore, the distribution of D.M.V.s in Somerset may represent the areas in which field work has taken place, but with this limitation in mind, a relatively superficial study indicates certain common geological factors. Research in other areas, e.g. Warwickshire, seems to indicate that economic and social factors were at least as important as topographical ones in influencing the course of settlement (personal communication, C.J. Bond). This may equally apply to Somerset.

Somerset D.M.V.s is clearly a subject which offers great scope to the archaeologist and historian. More fieldwork would undoubtedly reveal new sites which may radically alter any conclusions drawn from Fig. 8. More sites need to be excavated in order to draw conclusions about building types, and to trace the origin, growth and decline of each settlement. Finally, the archaeological evidence would have to be combined with documentary research to build up a picture of the medieval settlement of Somerset.

CONCLUSIONS

Excavations at Barrow Mead have revealed the changes in the plan and function of a 13th-14th century stone house, and shown that it succeeded an earlier stone house and timber buildings. The finds illustrate some of the activities carried out on the site, both agricultural and domestic, and suggest

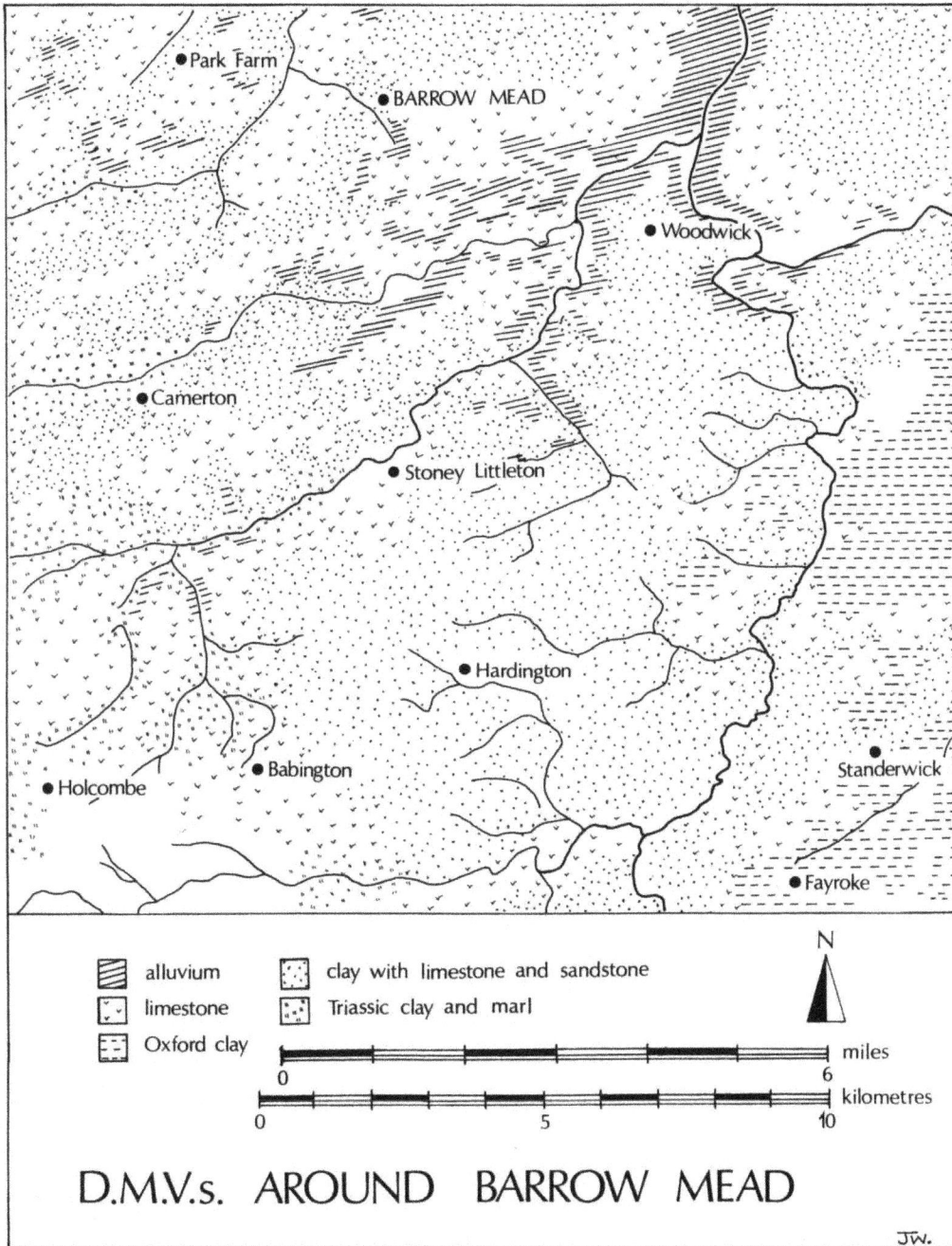

Park Farm

● BARROW MEAD

● Woodwick

● Camerton

● Stoney Littleton

● Hardington

● Standerwick

● Holcombe ● Babington

● Fayroke

▨	alluvium	⠂⠂	clay with limestone and sandstone
⌄⌄	limestone	⠒⠒	Triassic clay and marl
⠿	Oxford clay		

N

0   6 miles

0   5   10 kilometres

D.M.V.s. AROUND BARROW MEAD

JW.

FIG. 9

there was little contact with distant places. The site is important locally because it is one of the few excavations of a D.M.V. in Somerset. Some of the results however, the change from timber to stone construction, and from long house to farm house, are applicable on the national level. Because of the limited excavation, the results, though significant, must remain isolated from the whole context of medieval settlement and environment on the site.

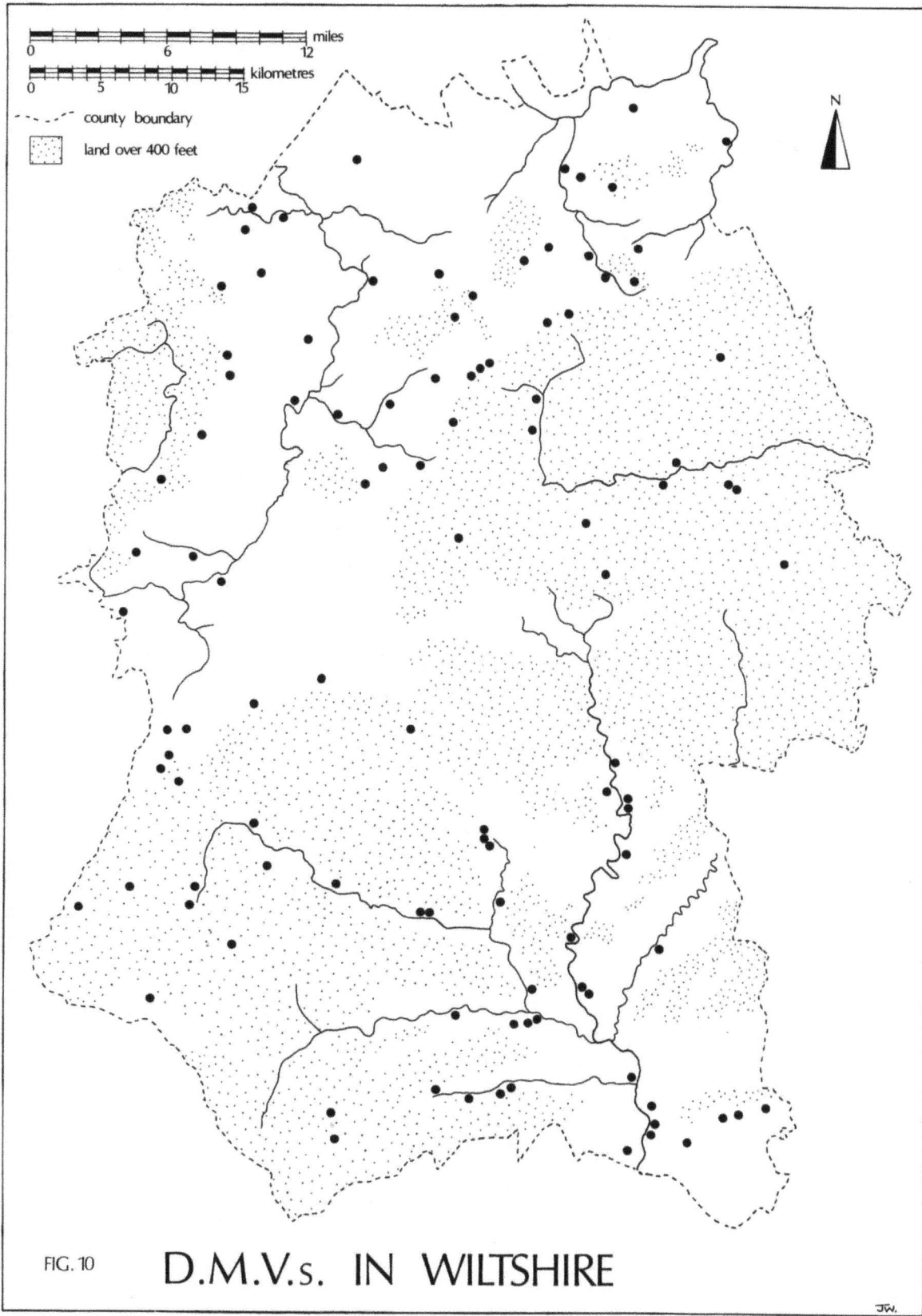

FIG. 10   D.M.V.s IN WILTSHIRE

FINDS DETAILS

(provenance and period in brackets after each; for correlation of finds see Appendix, p.52.

STONE (Fig. 11). Scientific examination by S. E. Ellis, British Museum (Natural History).

NB. "fr" - fragment.

1. Hone, broken one end, uneven wear, sharpening grooves (F52; IIIB2).
2. Hone, even wear, sharpening groove (F55; IIIB).

Not illustrated:

Fr. hone $3\frac{1}{4}$ x $1\frac{1}{2}$ x $\frac{1}{2}$-1 ins, even wear (F54; IIIB4).
Fr. hone $1\frac{1}{2}$ x $\frac{1}{2}$ x $\frac{1}{2}$ ins, even wear (T1).
Fr. hone $1\frac{1}{4}$ x $\frac{3}{4}$ x $\frac{3}{4}$ ins, even wear (F45; IIIB).
Fr. hone 2 x 1 x $\frac{1}{2}$ ins, even wear (F56; ?IIIB).

The collection of hones is noteworthy for the complete absence of the "Schist-hones" of Norwegian origin which make up the majority of hones on medieval sites in NE and south coastal areas and in the east and south Midlands; it is reminiscent of Romano-British rather than medieval sites.

The honestones are all impure, ill-sorted sandstones or siltstones (greywackes and sub-greywackes) of continental slope facies and although not identical are so much alike as to be probably from the same geological formation in the same district. They are rather lacking in distinctive characters which might enable one to decide positively between the several possible provenances, but most of these can be eliminated on historical-geographical grounds (e.g. S. Scotland, Central Wales, Brittany, the Rhineland). The nearest and most probable provenance is the Carboniferous, possibly also the Devonian, of NW Devon, and NE Cornwall, especially the Taw-Torridge estuary hinterland and the coast west and SW of this. Although this is at least 100 miles from Bath, it would have been quite accessible in terms of coastal trade even in the 13th and 14th centuries. It is possible that slates were regularly imported from this region, just as they were brought from south Devon to London and the South-East. The next nearest alternative provenance, Central Wales, seems much less probable.

3. Spindle-whorl, lathe incised (F52; IIIB2).
4. Spindle-whorl, lathe incised (F52; IIIB2).

Nos. 3 and 4 are compact, very fine-grained, pure limestone (calcite-mudstones). The most probable source is the "Chinastone" bands in the Carboniferous Limestone of the Avon gorge and the neighbouring country including the Mendip Hills. Somewhat similar calcite-mudstones also occur in the

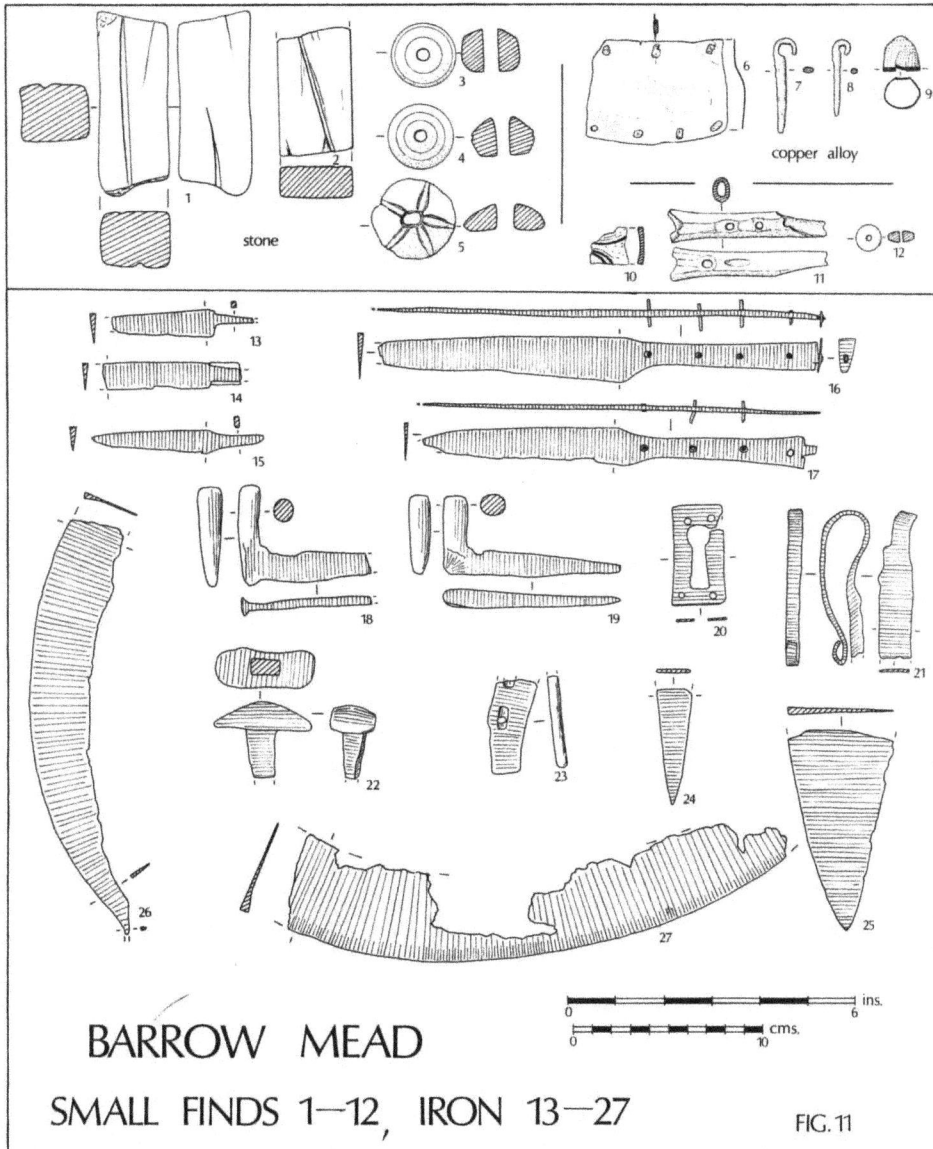

stone

copper alloy

BARROW MEAD

SMALL FINDS 1—12, IRON 13—27

FIG. 11

Lias where it abuts on the Mendips (e.g. at Shepton Mallet and probably also on the north side). The provenance is therefore likely to be local.

5. Spindle-whorl, re-used fossil sea-urchin of the cake-urchin type, determined by Dr. R. P. S. Jeffries of the British Museum (Natural History) as Pygurus sp. from the Great (Bath) Oolite series. Such fossils often occur locally as surface stones and are unlikely to have been brought from very far away (F52; IIIB2).

Not illustrated:

Stone disc 3¼ ins diameter, 1 in thick, sharpening groove. This is one of the rubbly reef limestones ('grits' or 'ragstones') which occur as beds in the Middle Jurassic of the Cotswold area. It is composed largely of fossil fragments mostly converted into small pisoliths by algal precipitation, but none are determinable so that the actual bed cannot be identified; but it is likely to be quite local (F45; IIIB).

JET (Fig. 11)

12. Jet bead (packing F41; IIIB).

BURNT CLAY

One piece of burnt daub (ashy area to NE of F19; IIC).

GLASS (Fig. 11)

10. Fr. vessel glass, inlaid black curved markings (F44; IIIB).

IRON (Fig. 11). Report by Ian H. Goodall.
(* denotes finds which have been X-radiographed).

*13. Knife, blade and whittle tang incomplete (F4; IIB).
*14. Knife, blade and whittle tang incomplete, with ferrified wood of handle (drawn in outline) on latter (F52; IIIB2).
*15. Knife, whittle tang incomplete (T1).
*16. Knife, blade incomplete, four iron rivets in scale tang which has a copper alloy end-cap held on a small nib formed by cutting away the end of the tang (F60; IIIB).
*17. Knife, blade tip lost, iron rivets preserved in three of the four holes in the scale tang which has a nib for a missing end-cap (F60; IIIB).

Knives

Occupation at Barrow Mead covered the period during which the scale tang knife was introduced, and knives with both whittle and scale tangs have been found. Of the whittle tang knives, nos. 13 & 15 with their equally tapering blades are examples of the most common type of medieval knife blade. The scale tang knives, nos. 16 & 17, are of considerable interest since both have a shoulder, a feature far more usually found on whittle tang knives.

18,19.   Hinge pivots, no. 18 with incomplete tang, but both with clear grooves worn by the turning of the hinge. The base of the guide arm of no. 18 has been burred by repeated hammering, no doubt to secure it more firmly in the wooden jamb (no. 18: F35; no. 19: F4; both IIB).

*20.   Keyhole escutcheon, four holes for the securing rivets, non-ferrous plating overall. The key entry has a splayed base, but a medieval shield-shaped escutcheon plate with a regularly shaped key entry is known from Brandon Castle, Warks. (Chatwin, 1955, 81, Fig. 11, no. 10), (T1).

21.   Distorted, rectangular sectioned strip, possibly part of the mechanism of a lock (F4; IIB).

22.   Stud with raised rectangular head and incomplete tang. A smaller example is known from Weoley Castle, Warks. (Oswald, 1962-3. 132, Fig. 51, no. 29), (below F35; IIB).

23.   Horseshoe tip, no calkin, with countersunk nailholes and wavy edge (below F58; IIIB2).

*24.   Probable blade tip of rectangular section but without any cutting edge (F33; IIIA).

25.   Tip of large shears blade (F44; IIIB).

26.   Sickle, whittle tang and blade incomplete. The blades of medieval sickles generally curve sharply away from the tang, but one from the late medieval site of Cambokeels, Co. Durham more closely resembles that from Barrow Mead (Hildyard, 1949, 199, Fig. 3, no. 22), (T1).

*27.   Scythe blade fragment with thickened back (T1).

COPPER ALLOY (Fig. 11). Report by Ian H. Goodhall.

6.   Distorted sheet metal patch with solid-headed rivets in six of the seven holes (T1).

7,8.   Buckle pins (no. 7: F45; no. 8: F44; both IIIB).

9.   Damaged thimble. For a discussion of the development of the medieval and post-medieval thimble see Moorhouse, 1971, 60 (T1).

COIN

Roman: AE3 house of Constantine, Gloria Exercitus (1 standard), 335-341 A.D. very worn, (among packing of F41; IIIB).

WORKED BONE (Fig. 11)

11.   Whistle, broken, carved from sheep or deer metatarsal, three finger holes, and thumb hole on reverse side, c.f. one from Canterbury, made from the long bone of a large bird, three finger holes, 12th or 13th century; one from White Castle, made from a deer metatarsal, five finger holes and two thumb holes, second half 13th century (Megaw, 1968, 149-50), (F45; IIIB).

ANIMAL REMAINS

Eggshell frs. (F50; IIIB1).

MOLLUSCS

Shells of cockles and mussels (F50; IIIB1).

POTTERY (for dating see p. 16)

Pottery was collected from each layer and feature, and recorded on site by the fabric series shown in Table 1. A total of 263 sherds were recovered, not including an almost complete glazed jug. The majority are 13th-14th century, but there are also some Iron Age, Roman and post-medieval sherds. All rim, base and decorated sherds were retained, and the rest were discarded on site: none from the group "medieval glazed" were kept. 185 sherds were available for study. These showed that in the case of "miscellaneous cooking pot", the original grouping had been too general, as it was possible to divide the remaining 68 sherds into at least seven types, A-F (Table 2). Groups L and M were also subdivided. Although many of the groupings made on site were confirmed, it is possible that some significant sherds may have been discarded. The final type-fabric series is described below. From a total of eighteen main groups (not including sub-divisions) ten include less than ten sherds. Two groups (D and E) are composed of only one sherd. Therefore the majority of the pottery falls into eight fabric groups. Such a wide variety of fabrics are represented in this comparatively small quantity of pottery that the series is capable of almost limitless expansion. Sherds have therefore been included under the heading "miscellaneous" when they cannot be fitted into any of the main groups.

This analysis of the pottery into type-fabrics has considerable limitations. Sorting was carried out on the basis of appearance only, and without any scientific examinations. As a result, sherds that appear similar may be totally unrelated, while sherds assigned to different groups may be of similar date and origin. Many differences may be the result of variable firing conditions. Some sherds could not be fitted into a fabric type, while others showed characteristics of two or more groups. This method of sorting is also completely subjective: there is the strong possibility that another person would have divided the Barrow Mead pottery into different groups.

In spite of its limitations however, such an analysis enables pottery to be classified into a coherent pattern, which makes comparison with other sites much easier. It is not suggested that the type-fabrics have any cultural or chronological significance.

The pottery was examined by Alan G. Vince, and some sherds selected for further study. The results are given in a specialist report on p. 51.

The Type-fabrics

NB. grits are called "quartzite" (very hard shiny), "limestone" (grey matt stoney), "white" (uncertain); "sandy" fabrics have a sandy feel and grits too small to be seen by eye; "pitted" sherds are usually those with grits weathered or burnt out. (This corresponds to the definitions used at

TABLE 1: Site Analysis of Pottery by Fabric (letters of final type-fabrics in brackets)

Features	1	4	5	12	14	18	27	29	30	31	33	35	37	41	44	45	49	56	55	50	52	53	D	58	59	54	E	60	T1	T2	Total	%
Misc. cooking pot (A–D, F–G)	3	6	2	–	–	4	1	10	1	2	1	1	1	–	8	3	3	2	4	5	11	5	–	2	–	1	2	–	1	–	79	30.0
Black, white gritted with 'fried' glaze (E)	1	–	–	–	–	–	–	–	–	–	–	–	–	–	–	–	–	–	–	–	–	–	–	–	–	–	–	–	–	–	1	–
Misc. glazed (H)	1	6	–	3	4	–	–	–	–	2	–	–	–	1	1	3	3	3	1	–	1	1	–	–	–	1	1	–	2	2	38	14.4
Medieval glazed (I)	4	2	1	–	1	–	1	1	–	–	1	1	1	–	1	2	3	8	2	3	6	3	1	–	1	2	1	–	5	1	49	18.6
Polychrome glazed (J)	–	1	–	–	–	–	–	–	–	–	–	–	–	–	1	–	1	1	1	–	–	–	–	–	–	1*	–	–	–	–	6	2.3
Salmon-pink fabric with purplish glaze (K)	1	–	–	–	–	–	–	–	–	–	–	–	–	–	–	–	–	–	–	–	–	–	–	–	–	–	–	3	–	–	4	1.5
Hard off-white (L)	–	1	–	–	–	1	1	1	–	–	–	–	–	–	2	–	–	1	–	–	–	–	–	–	–	–	1	–	3	2	11	4.2
Off-white, all over green glaze (M)	–	3	–	–	–	–	–	–	–	–	–	–	–	–	–	1	–	1	–	–	–	–	–	–	–	2	–	–	2	–	9	3.4
Grey, white gritted (NI)	–	1	2	–	–	1	–	–	–	–	1	–	–	–	2	–	–	–	–	–	1	–	–	–	1	–	–	–	–	–	8	3.0

TABLE 1: Site Analysis of Pottery by Fabric (letters of final type-fabrics in brackets)

Features	1	4	5	12	14	18	27	29	30	31	33	35	37	41	44	45	49	56	55	50	52	53	D	58	59	54	E	60	T1	T2	Total	%
Grey, white gritted glazed (NII)	-	2	-	-	-	-	-	-	-	-	1	-	-	-	-	1	-	-	-	-	-	-	-	-	-	-	-	-	2	-	6	2.3
Ham green (O)	-	3	-	4	-	-	-	-	-	-	1	-	-	-	4	1	-	-	-	-	-	-	-	-	-	-	-	-	3	1	17	6.5
Iron age (IR.A)	20	1	-	-	-	-	-	-	-	-	-	-	-	-	-	-	-	-	-	-	-	-	-	-	-	-	-	-	-	1	22	8.4
Roman coarse (RO.I)	4	-	-	-	-	-	-	-	-	-	-	-	-	-	-	-	1	-	-	-	-	-	-	-	-	-	-	-	-	-	5	1.9
Samian (RO.II)	-	-	-	-	-	-	-	-	-	-	-	-	-	-	-	-	-	-	-	-	-	-	-	-	1	-	1	-	1	-	3	1.1
Post-medieval (P-MED)	-	-	-	-	-	-	-	-	1	-	-	-	-	-	-	-	-	-	-	-	-	-	-	-	-	-	-	-	4	-	5	1.9
Totals	34	26	5	7	5	4	1	13	1	4	4	2	1	1	19	11	11	15	9	8	18	10	2	4	1	5	9	2	22	9	263	

D: Disturbance through F54 to F52.

E: Pottery recorded from exterior of IIIB stone house, south of entrance.

*: Almost complete jug, not included in totals.

TABLE 2

Final Analysis by Fabric of "Misc. Cooking Pot"

	1	4	5	12	14	18	27	29	30	31	33	35	37	41	44	45	49	56	55	50	52	53	D	58	59	54	E	60	T1	T2	Total
AI																		1	1												2
AII								1								1	1	1		1	1	2					1		1		10
B	1																			1	3						1				6
C										1					1	1															3
D																			1												1
E	1																														1
F	1							1																							2
G	2	5	1			4		8		1					4	2	2		2	3	7	3				1					43
Total	5	5	1			4		10		2					5	2	3	2	4	5	11	5				1	2		1		68

Cheddar; Rahtz, 1964, 205). A "fried" glaze has an opaque, fine bubbly surface.

A   **Fine hard black micaceous.** A well-known fabric in the area, common at Cheddar (fabric J) in the 12th-13th centuries, and found on many local sites including CVL., Bristol, etc.

            I   typical
            II rough

B   Hard buff surfaces with white grits.

C   Fine hard sandy.

D   Hard sandy (one sherd).

E   Black, white gritted with fried glaze (one sherd).

F   Black soapy limestone gritted; similar to some pre-Conquest fabrics at Cheddar.

G   Miscellaneous cooking pot.

H   Miscellaneous glazed.

I   Medieval glazed; discarded on site, no information available.

J   Polychrome glazed.

K   Salmon-pink fabric with pink-buff surfaces and purplish looking glaze.

L   Hard off-white, turned on fast wheel; local copies of foreign imports (personal communication J. G. Hurst). This group of eleven sherds covers a wide range of fabrics.

            I   with "fried" glaze (not illustrated).
            II with spots of green looking glaze.
            III with all-over lemon-green looking glaze.

M   Coarse off-white with all-over green looking glaze; body sherds on only, not represented in the illustrated series.

            I   glazed inside, 14th century.
            II glazed outside.

N   Grey, white gritted, buff soapy surface: Selsley Common type, 13th century.

            I   unglazed.
            II glazed.

O   Ham Green type.

IR.A.   Iron Age

RO.   Roman

            I   coarse ware.
            II samian.

P-MED Post Medieval.

DISCUSSION

Out of 156 medieval sherds retained from the excavation, a minimum of c. 100 pots are represented. This suggests that the majority of broken pottery, with the exception of one glazed jug, was dispersed outside the excavated area.

Glazed sherds account for 62% of the medieval pottery. This compares with 40% + from CVL. and only 4.6% from Holworth. Such a high proportion may be the result of the small sample of pottery analysed, but it serves to emphasise the difficulties of assessing social stratification from the proportions of glazed ware.

The majority of the Iron Age and Roman pottery comes from F1. Four out of five post-medieval sherds are from the topsoil. The density of medieval pottery is fairly uniform throughout periods II and III. Most of the sherds came from occupation levels or features; very few were found in the walls of the stone buildings. All but one sherd of type K come from the topsoil.

Apart from the sherds of Ham Green type and those with affinities to Lacock's Green ware, no kiln sources for the pottery can be given yet. It is clear however that the sherds are of local and Cotswold types, and that Barrow Mead was not receiving pottery from more distant sources.

Any discussion of the significance of the material from Barrow Mead is hampered by the absence of any general survey of local pottery. The information is contained in individual site reports, and is dependent on the excavators own interpretation of fabric, form and context. A paper which attempted to bring together the pottery from the Bristol area would enable type-fabrics to be placed in a wider context, and their chronological value to be assessed.

ILLUSTRATED POTTERY (Figs. 12-15)

87 sherds have been drawn, which include all rims and bases. These have been arranged in associated groups. The majority of the vessels are represented by only one sherd, which makes it impossible to draw many conclusions about form. Cooking pots were the most common vessel, followed by jugs and bowls. Two sagging bases are represented, as well as lids and/or shallow dishes. It can be said that the rims vary considerably in diameter, and are on the whole simple and undeveloped.

NB. the following abbreviations are used: "sh" (sherd), "C.P." (cooking pot), "gl" (glazed). The type-fabric letter is in brackets at the end of each description. * denotes sherds selected by Vince for further examination (see pottery report

1-5 from F1, periods IA & B, IIA.

1. Rim sh. of C.P., hard dark grey, white and few quartzite grits, buff surfaces (IR.A.).
2. Rim sh. of C.P., coarse light grey, quartzite grits, buff surfaces (IR.A.).
3. Rim sh. of C.P., hard black, white gritted, smooth surfaces (IR.A.).
4. Rim sh. of C.P., hard dark grey, white grits, red inner surface, black outer surface (IR.A.).
5. Rim sh. of C.P., diameter uncertain, brown with red surfaces (RO.I).

Not illustrated:

* Body sh. of C.P., outer surface has thin black skin on red margin - a feature characteristic of some pre-Conquest fabrics at Cheddar (F).
* Body sh. of C.P., buff pitted inner surface (E).

FIG. 12

Iron Age ditch

Timber buildings

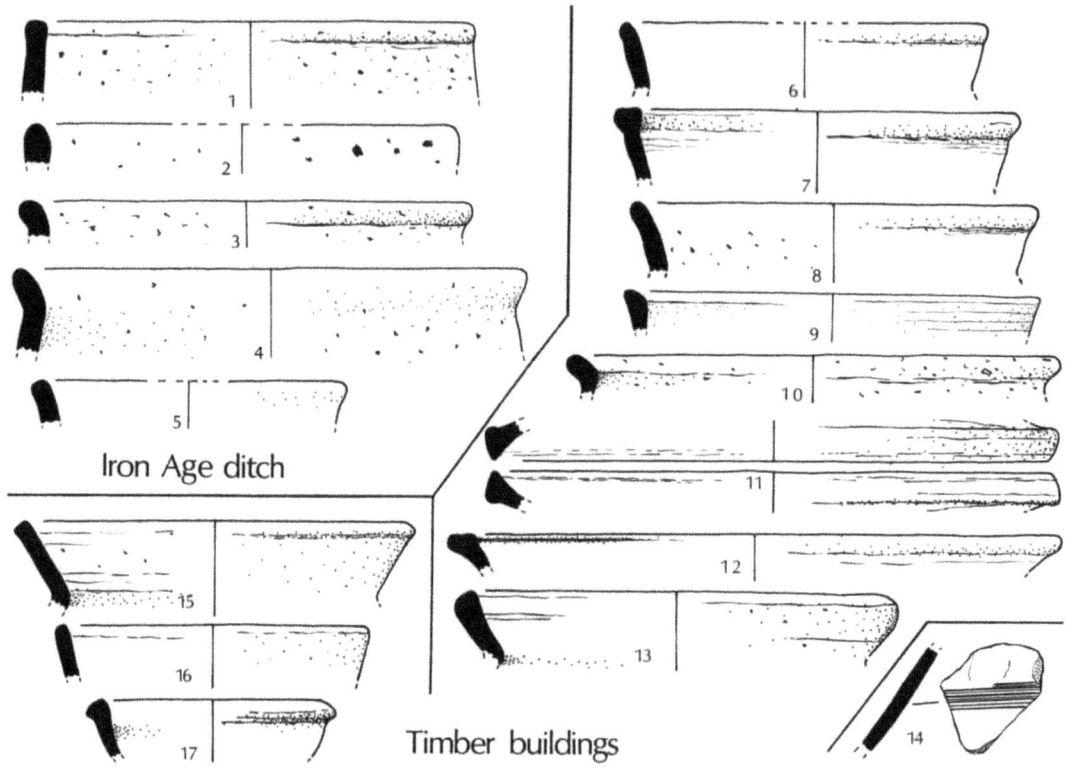

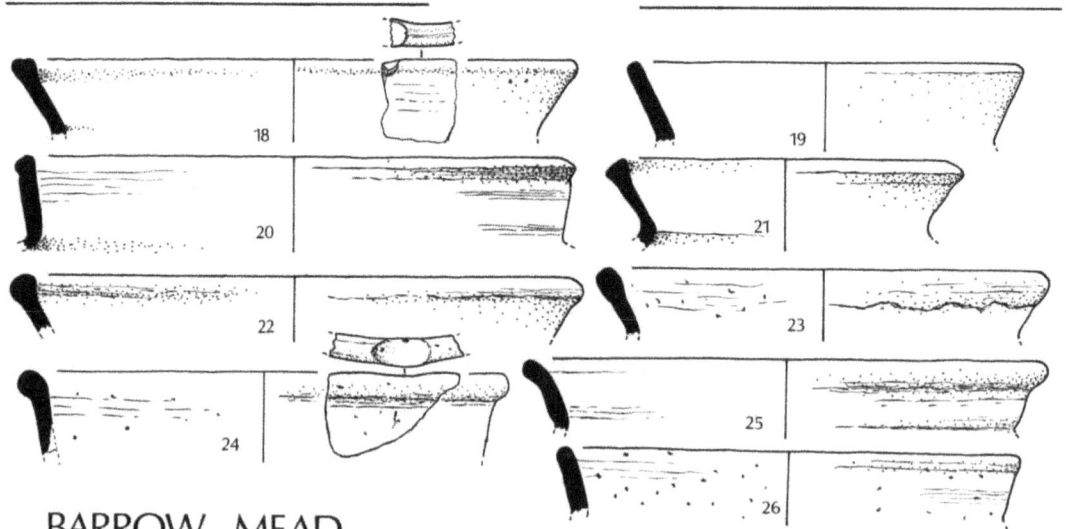

BARROW MEAD
POTTERY 1–26

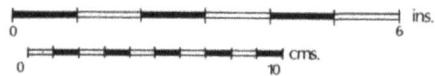

ins.

cms.

Jw.

6-13 from F4, period IIB.

*6.   Rim sh. of C.P., diameter uncertain, coarse grey micaceous, quartzite grits, dark buff surfaces (G).

7.   Rim sh. of C.P., coarse grey micaceous, quartzite and few white grits, buff surfaces, may be Cotswold type with almost vertical sides and clubbed rim, C. F. Jope 1952 (G).

8.   Rim sh. of C.P., coarse brown, quartzite and white grits (G).

9.   Rim sh. of C.P., fine hard light grey, few quartzite grits, grey to buff surfaces, patches of green looking glaze on outside (H).

10.   Rim sh. of C.P., fine hard black, white grits, black to brown surfaces (IR.A.).

11.   Lid sh., or may be rim of platter or shallow bowl, fine hard light grey, quartzite grits, orange surfaces (G)·

12.   Rim sh. of C.P., or bowl, coarse hard light grey, quartzite grits, orange to black surfaces, c.f. Lacock's Green (G).

*13.   Rim sh. of C.P., traces of green looking glaze on inside, oxidized, 14th-15th century (NII).

Not illustrated:

*   Base of strap handle (NI).

*   Sagging base sh. of C.P., smooth surfaces, traces of green looking gl. on inside (NII).

    Body sh. of jug, fine gritty light grey, green looking gl. on outside, painted white stripe (J).

14 from F5, period IIB.

*14.   Body sh. of C.P., quartzite grits, inner surface buff to brown and pitted, outer surface grey to black, pimply, with incised girth grooves, c.f. Selsley Common Fig. 2, nos. 4-6. (NI).

15-17 from F18, period IIC.

15.   Rim sh. of C.P., coarse hard grey, quartzite grits, buff surfaces (G).

16.   Rim sh. of C.P., fabric similar to 15 (G).

17.   Rim sh. of bowl, coarse grey micaceous quartzite and white grits, buff surfaces (G).

18-26 from F29, period IIC.

18.   Rim sh. of C.P., quartzite grits (AII).

19.   Rim sh. of C.P., fabric similar to 15 (G).

20.   Rim shs. of C.P., coarse grey micaceous, large white and some quartzite grits, dark grey to buff surfaces, c.f. CVL., Fig. 116, no. 21; 12th century (G).

21.   Rim sh. of C.P., coarse grey, quartzite and large white grits, buff to black surfaces (G).

22.   Rim sh. of bowl, coarse grey micaceous, quartzite grits, light buff surfaces, c.f. CVL., Fig. 116, no. 15; late 12th-early 13th century (G).

23.   Rim sh. of C.P., coarse grey micaceous, quartzite grits, black to dark buff surfaces (G).

24. Rim sh. of C.P., coarse grey micaceous, quartzite and white grits, light buff surfaces (G).

25. Rim sh. of C.P., fine grey micaceous, quartzite grits, buff surfaces (G).

*26. Rim sh. of C.P., handmade and partly oxidized, top and inside has thin black skin on red margin - a feature characteristic of some pre-Conquest fabrics at Cheddar (F).

27-28 from F31, period IIIA.

27. Rim sh. of C.P., coarse hard brown, few quartzite grits (G).
28. Rim sh. of C.P., brown micaceous (C).

29-33 from F55, period IIIB.

29. Rim sh. of C.P., coarse grey micaceous, large quartzite grits, buff surfaces (G).

30. Rim sh. of C.P., hard grey micaceous, quartzite and white grits, buff surfaces (G).

31. Body sh. of jug, grey, quartzite grits, inner surface off-white, lemon-green looking glaze and combed decoration on outer surface (LIII).

32. Rim sh. of C.P., red micaceous, turned on fast wheel, c.f. Upton 1966, Fig. 17, no. 31, and Lacock's Green (D).

33. Sagging base sh. of C.P., few quartzite and fine white grits, brown inner surface (AI).

Not illustrated:

Body sh. of jug, fine light grey, quartzite grits, inner surface light buff pitted, mottled green looking glaze on outside, dark stripes are possibly variations in the glaze (J).

34-39 from F45, period IIIB.

*34. Rim sh. of C.P., traces of green looking glaze on inside, oxidized, 14th-15th century (NII).

35. Rim sh. of C.P., coarse grey micaceous, quartzite grits, red surfaces, patches of fried glaze on inside; rim form paralleled at Upton 1969, e.g. Fig. 122, no. 105, but in different fabrics (H).

*36. Rim sh. of jug, coarse grey, white grits, light buff surfaces, traces of green looking glaze on outside, c.f. Glastonbury, Fig. 30, no. 39 (H).

37. Rim sh. of C.P., coarse grey quartzite grits, grey outer surface on orange margin, c.f. Cheddar thesis, Fig. 85, no. 162 (AII).

38. Body sh. of jug, hard buff sandy with grey core, all-over light green glaze, applied thumb-pressed decoration; Ham Green (O).

39. Sagging base sh. of C.P., grey micaceous, quartzite and white grits, brown surfaces (C).

40-48 from F44, period IIIB.

40. Rim sh. of large bowl, grey micaceous, white grits, buff to black surfaces (G).

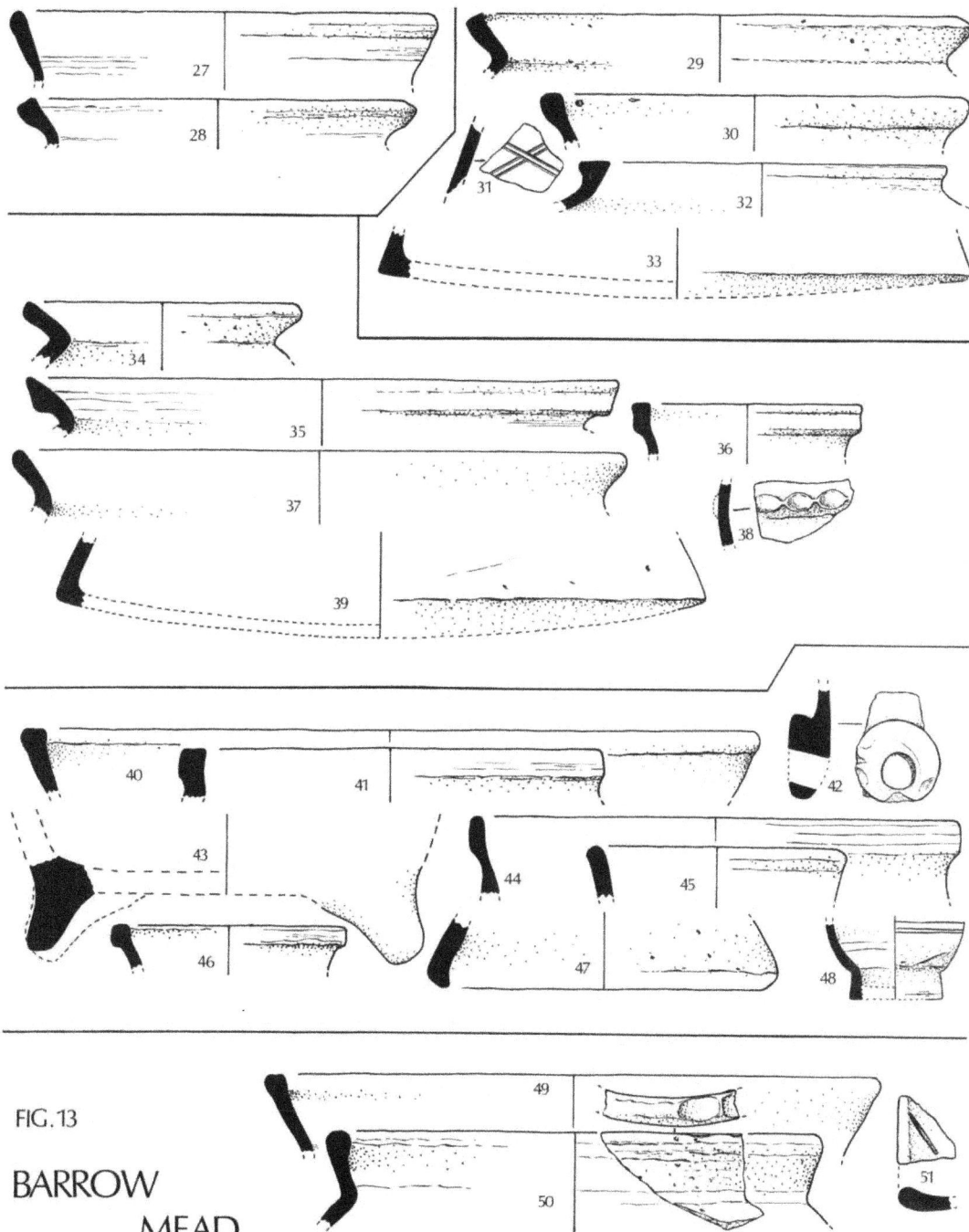

FIG. 13

BARROW
     MEAD
STONE HOUSE POTTERY 27–51

Jw.

41. Rim sh. of C.P., buff micaceous, quartzite and fine white grits, brown surfaces (C).

*42. Bung-hole from jar, quartzite grits, pitted surfaces, oxidized, late medieval, ? 15th century (NI).

*43. Foot of tripod pitcher, fine light grey, light buff to grey oxidized surfaces, c.f. CVL., Fig. 117, no. 45; late 12th-early 13th century (NI).

44. Rim sh. of C.P., coarse grey micaceous, quartzite and white grits, buff inner surface, buff outer surface on off-white margin (G).

45. Rim shs. of C.P., grey quartzite grits, buff to off-white surfaces, c.f. Back Hall, Fig. 7, no. 4 (L).

46. Rim sh. of jug, coarse grey, large quartzite and fine white grits, light buff surfaces (G).

47. Sh. of lid, coarse grey, much eroded (G).

48. Base sh. of jug or cup, fine hard light grey, turned on fast wheel, all-over green mottled gl. inside and out (H).

Not illustrated:

Body sh. of jug, fine grey, quartzite grits, reddish-brown surfaces, traces of green looking gl., painted brown stripe (J).

49-51 from exterior of house south of entrance, period IIIB.

49. Rim sh. of C.P., grey, quartzite grits, buff inner surface (AII).

50. Rim sh. of C.P., coarse grey, quartzite grits, surfaces pitted, outer edge of rim black (B).

*51. Fr. of strap handle, dark buff surfaces, oblique slashed decoration (NI).

52-55 from F49, period IIIB.

52. Thumbed base sh. of C.P., form uncertain, fine hard grey, few quartzite grits, light buff surfaces, traces of green looking gl. on outside (H).

53. Lid, or rim sh. of platter or shallow bowl, grey white and quartzite grits, light grey inner surface, dark grey outer surface (AII).

54. Rim sh. of C.P., coarse black micaceous, large quartzite and white grits, dark grey surfaces, applied thumb-pressed strip (G).

55. Rim sh. of C.P., coarse grey, quartzite and fine white grits, buff surfaces, c.f. Baldwin St., Fig. 10, no. 11; possibly 12th century (G).

Not illustrated:

Body sh. of jug, fine grey, quartzite grits, inner surface buff, green looking gl. on outside, painted dark grey stripe (J).

56-58 from F50, period IIIB1.

56. Rim sh. of C.P., coarse grey micaceous, large quartzite and fine white grits, buff to black surfaces, c.f. CVL., Fig. 117, no. 34; late 12th or early 13th century (G).

FIG. 14

52

53

54

55

56

57

58

59

60

61

62

63

64

65

66

67

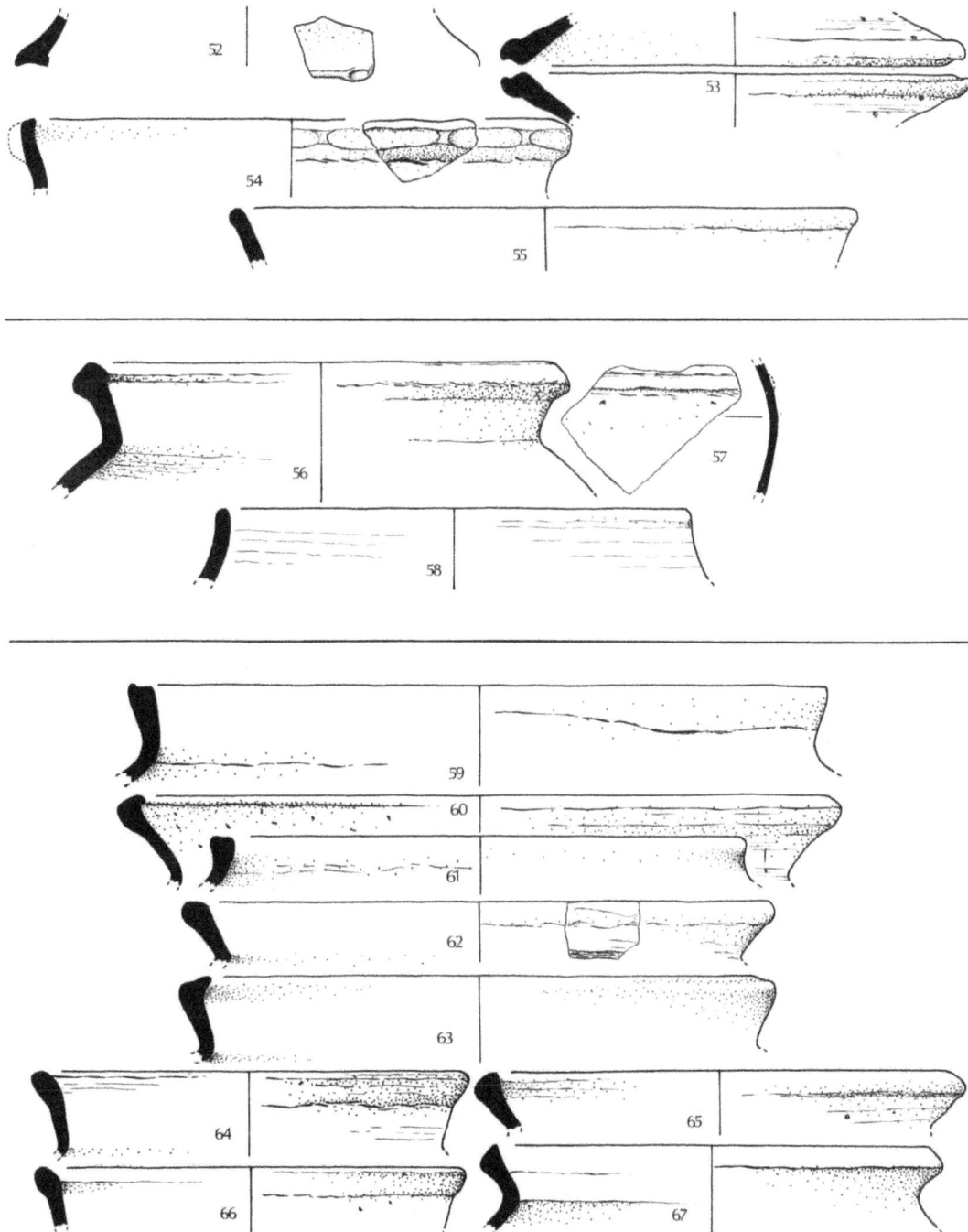

BARROW MEAD
STONE HOUSE POTTERY 52-67

0 ins. 6

0 cms. 10

Jw.

57. Body sh. of C.P., coarse grey, quartzite and white grits, buff to black inner surface, buff outer surface with applied strip of same clay and incised decoration (G).

58. Rim sh. of C.P., grey, quartzite grits, turned on fast wheel, inner surface light grey, brown to black outer surface (AII).

59-67 from F52, period IIIB2.

59. Rim shs. of C.P., coarse grey, very large quartzite and few white grits, light buff to black surfaces (G).

60. Rim sh. of C.P., coarse grey, quartzite grits (B).

61. Rim sh. of C.P., quartzite grits, grey outer surface, c.f. Cheddar thesis, Fig. 85, no. 156, (AII).

62. Rim sh. of C.P., fine grey micaceous, quartzite and fine white grits, buff surfaces (G).

63. Rim sh. of C.P., grey, quartzite and fine white grits, black inner surface, black to grey outer surface, c.f. Cheddar thesis, Fig. 85, no. 155 (AII).

64. Rim sh. of C.P., coarse grey micaceous, buff surfaces (G).

65. Rim sh. of C.P., coarse grey micaceous, quartzite grits, buff surfaces (G).

66. Rim sh. of C.P., coarse grey, quartzite and white grits, brown surfaces (G).

67. Rim sh. of C.P., coarse grey, quartzite grits, buff to black surfaces (G).

68-71 from F53, period IIIB2.

68. Lid sh., hard grey micaceous, quartzite grits, turned on fast wheel, fine light grey surfaces (G).

69. Rim sh. of C.P., grey gritty, buff to black inner surface, orange, buff and black outer surface (AII).

70. Rim sh. of C.P., coarse grey, quartzite grits, black inner surface, buff outer surface (G).

*71. Fr. of strap handle, fine light grey, light buff oxidized surfaces, oblique slashed decoration, late medieval ? 15th century (NI).

72-74 from F54, period IIIB4.

72. Most of bridge-spouted jug, fine hard red with grey core, all-over green looking gl. mottled on outside, fried on inside, applied strips of reddish-brown clay appear to form a spiral motif but adjoining body shs. missing, handle has two thumb markings at the base. Decoration and fabric are paralleled at Lacock's Green, although the jugs are usually larger (J).

73. Rim sh. of jug, coarse grey, quartzite grits, buff to brown surfaces, traces of green looking gl. on outside, c.f. CVL., Fig. 118, no. 65 (H).

74. Rim sh. of C.P., coarse grey micaceous, turned on fast wheel, buff surfaces (G).

Not illustrated:

Body sh. of jug, grey gritty, reddish surfaces, green-looking gl., painted white stripe, c.f. Upton 1966, Fig. 135, no. 52 (J).

FIG.15

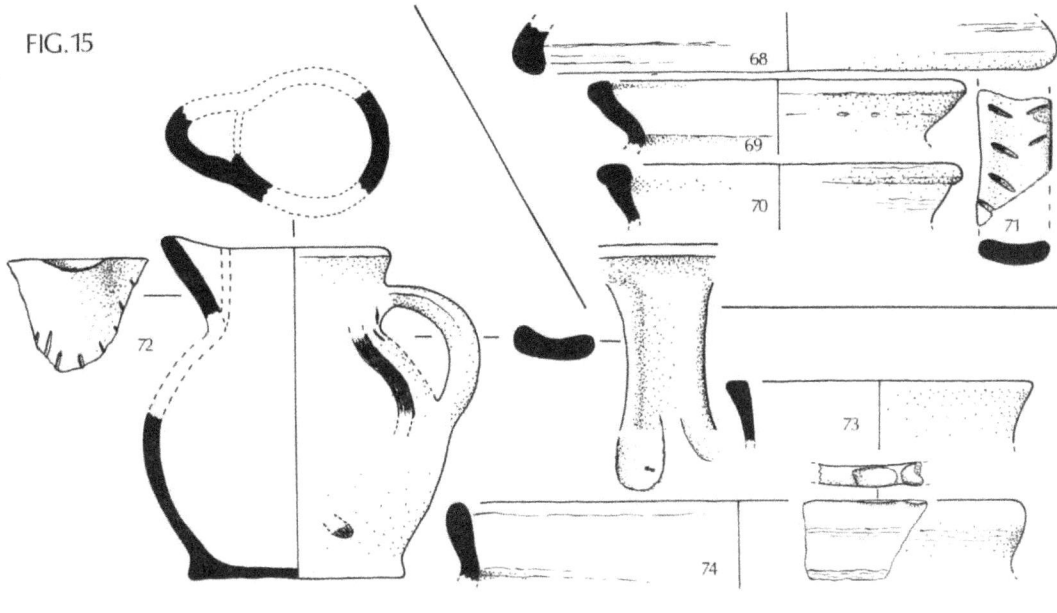

Stone house
68-81

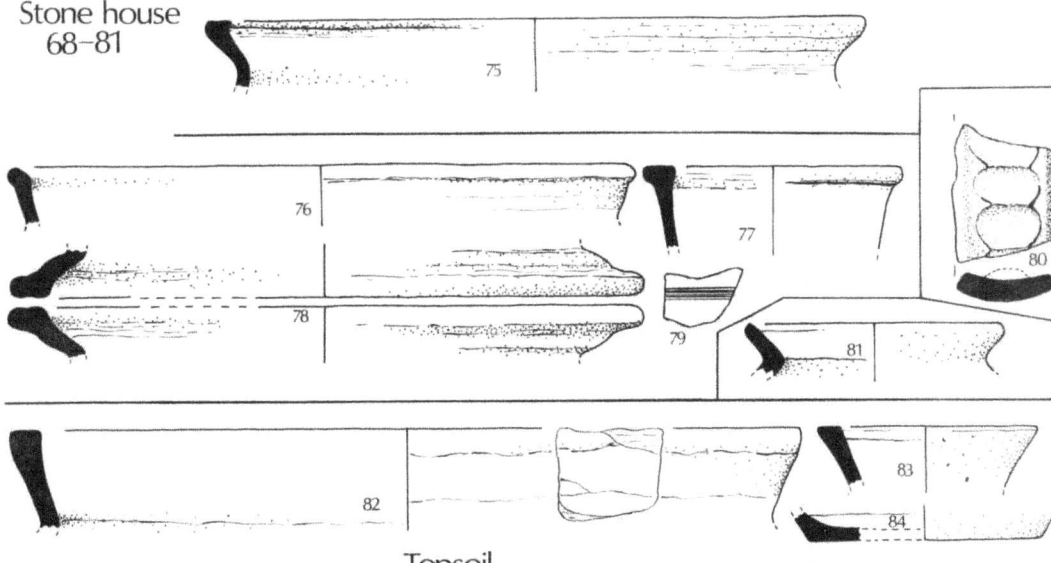

Topsoil

BARROW MEAD
POTTERY 68-87

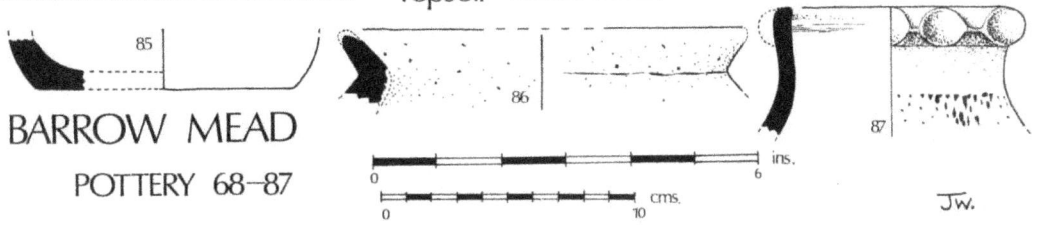

0   6
ins.

0   10
cms.

Jw.

75 from disturbance through F54 to F52.

75.   Rim sh. of C.P., hard grey, quartzite grits, turned on fast wheel,
      dark brown surfaces on orange margin, traces of ? colourless gl.
      outside and inside, c.f. Upton 1966, Fig. 16, no. 14 (unglazed) (H).

76-79 from F56, period IIIB.

76.   Rim sh. of C.P., quartzite and white grits, grey to brown inner sur-
      face, black to brown outer surface (AII).
77.   Rim sh. of jug, fine hard light grey, buff surfaces, traces of green
      looking gl. on outside (H).
78.   Lid, or may be rim sh. of shallow bowl or platter, diameter uncer-
      tain but more than 10 ins, few quartzite and fine white grits, turned
      on fast wheel, brown surface on outer lip (AI).
79.   Body sh. of jug, soft red sandy with grey core, green looking gl. on
      outside, combed decoration (H).

Not illustrated:

      Body sh. of jug, fine grey, inner surface buff, green looking gl. on
      outside, painted dark grey stripe (J).

80 from below F58, period IIIB3.

*80. Fr. of handle, coarse hard grey, not Oolitic limestone, abundant fine
      quartz sand, buff surfaces, traces of all-over green looking gl.,
      applied thumb-pressed strip in centre (H).

81 from F60, rubble period IIIB.

*81. Rim sh. of C.P., quartzite grits, traces of green looking gl. on
      inner and outer surfaces, oxidized, 14th-15th century (NII).

Not illustrated:

      * Sagging base sh. of C.P., traces of green looking gl. on inside
      (NII).

82-84 from T1.

82.   Rim sh. of C.P., brown outer surface, c.f. Cheddar thesis, Fig.
      85, no. 165 (AII).
83.   Rim sh. of jug, quartzite grits, buff outer surface with spots of
      green looking gl., c.f. Baldwin St., Fig. 19, no. 19 (LII).
84.   Base sh. of bowl or dish, grey core, quartzite grits, spots of green
      looking gl. on outside (LII).

85-87 from T2.

85.   Base shs. of C.P., traces of purplish looking gl. on outside (K).
86. · Rim sh. of C.P., coarse black, white grits (IR.A).
87.   Rim sh. of jug, hard grey, white grits, buff and pink surfaces, all-
      over dark green gl. on outside, applied and thumb-pressed decora-
      tion, rouletting on body; Ham Green (O).

Not illustrated:

      Base sh. of C.P., quartzite grits, brown outer surface with fried
      green looking gl. (LI).

POTTERY REPORT

Alan G. Vince

The pottery from Barrow Mead was searched by eye for sherds containing Oolitic limestone, and a number of sherds (marked in the text by an asterix) were removed to Southampton University for further study.

The material was examined on polished sections under x20 magnification, and the following inclusion types were recognised; crystalline calcite fragments, fossil shell, amorphous limestone and limestone fragments containing Ooliths (spherical objects with concentric structure). Occasional quartz grains were seen but were not common. Every sherd contained a proportion of Oolitic limestone.

Within the small group of pottery examined, every major form from the 10th/12th century through to the 15th century is present. This suggests that the Cotswold types form a small but consistent part of the ceramic assemblage at Barrow Mead throughout the medieval period. The possible sources of this material are numerous, but the similarity in form and technique in many cases suggests the same source as for the Cotswold types at Gloucester (Vince, forthcoming).

APPENDIX: LIST OF FEATURES

F.NO	INTERPRETATION	DESCRIPTION	FINDS *	PERIOD	FIG.	PAGE
1	ditch	see sections for stratigraphy	Iron Age, Roman and medieval pottery (Fig. 12, nos. 1-5)	IA, recut in IIA	2, 3, 5 (Sections CD, DF), **6** (Section BC)	6
2	uncertain	vertical sided, maximum depth 12 ins filled with clayey soil and many stones; below F4	–	pre IIB (see page ref.)	3, 5 (Section DF)	8
3	uncertain	10 ins deep, dark soil fill in bottom 6 ins; below F4	–	pre IIB (see page ref.)	3	8
4	metalling	small stones and brown earth 2-6 ins deep with maximum depth over F1; below F5 in part of North-West Trench	iron knife, hinge pivot & distorted strip (Fig. 17, nos. 13, 19, 21); pottery (Fig. 12, nos. 6-13), including one Iron Age sherd	IIB partly re-used in III	3, 4, 5 (Section CD) 6 (Sections AE, BC)	8
5	cobbles of a floor	large, compact cobbles, merging with F4 in the north of the excavated area, and overlying this layer in part of the North-West Trench	pottery (Fig. 12, no. 14)	IIB, partly re-used in III	3, 4, 6 (Sections AE, BC)	10

52

No.	Type	Description		Phase		
6	post hole	24 x 24 x 5 ins deep from F5 sloping sides, filled with greyish-brown soil; sealed by F14	–	IIB	3	10
7	2 post holes	3 x 3 x 1½ ins, and 6 x 6 x 2 ins deep from F5, filled with greyish-brown soil; sealed by F14	–	IIB	3	10
8	post hole	8 x 6 x 2 ins deep from F5, filled with greyish-brown soil; sealed by F14	–	IIB	3	10
9	post hole	5 x 6 x 3 ins deep from F5, filled with greyish-brown soil; sealed by F14	–	IIB	3	10
10	post hole	5 ins diameter, 3½ ins deep, dark soil fill with stones at the bottom; sealed by F14	–	IIB	3	10
11	drain	1½–3 ins deep from F5, filled with greyish-brown soil; sealed by F14	–	IIB	3	10
12	sump	2 ins deep from F5; sealed by F14	pottery	IIB	3,6 (section BC)	10
13	ditch	2 ft 6 ins deep, filled with brown clayey soil & small stones. This level is completely homo-genous without any signs of	–	IIB, recut in IIIB	3,4; Rahtz, 1960–1, Fig. 5	10,14

		silting and probably re-presents a deliberate back-filling. The ditch is later recut to a depth of 1 ft and filled with charcoal flecked brown soil				
14	destruction level	layer of dark brown clayey soil with small stones; lies directly above F5, & below F29; in North-West Trench covered by F45; seals features of period IIB	pottery	IIB	3, 6 (sections AE, BC)	10
15	hearth	local stones burnt powdery white; resurfaced with pennant sandstone, burnt grey, and clay; lies on F14: this layer and F5 below it burnt through; covered by F29	–	IIC	3	10
16	post hole	5 ins deep from F14	–	IIC	3, 6 (section AE)	10
17	post hole	6 ins deep, filled with dark soil, flat stone at the bottom; below F43.	–	IIC	3	10
18	latrine pit	12 ins deep, filled with mixed clay including green clay F29; sealed by F29	pottery (Fig. 12, nos. 15-17)	IIC	3	10

54

No.	Type	Description		Phase	Plan	
19	oven base	stones burnt powdery white; ashy area, presumably where raked out, to NE; lies on F14; partly covered by F29	piece of burnt daub	IIC	3	10
20	post hole	3 ins deep from F14, filled with dark soil; below F43	–	IIC	3,6 (section AE)	10
21	post hole	4 ins deep from F14, cuts through F5; layer of hard packed orange clay observed at base; below wall F59	–	IIC	2	10
22	post hole	12 ins deep from F14 filled with mixed black soil and greenish clay, three vertical slabs extending to base; sealed by F29	–	IIC	3	10
23	post hole	3 ins deep from F14, filled with black soil; sealed by F29	–	IIC	3	10
24	post hole	10 x 6 x 4 ins deep from F14; filled with dark soil, cobbles of F5 in base; below wall F58	–	IIC	3	10
25	post hole	$2\frac{1}{2}$ ins diameter, $2\frac{1}{2}$ ins deep from F14, filled with dark soil, cobbles of F5 in base; below wall F58	–	IIC	3	10

No.	Type	Description	Finds	Period		
26	post hole	6 x 10 x 3½ ins deep from F14 filled with dark soil, cobbles of F5 in base; below wall F58	–	IIC	3	10
27	post hole	5 ins diameter, 3 ins deep from F14, filled with dark soil and charcoal, packing stone on south side	one sherd pottery	IIC	3	10
28	uncertain	feature of unknown dimensions and function in 1954 section, 6 ins deep; sealed by F29	–	IIC	3, Rahtz 1960–1, Fig. 5	10
29	destruction level	two layers of green clay separated by a thin band of charcoal; above F14 below F50; seals features of period IIC	pottery (Fig. 12, nos. 18–26) including one post-medieval sherd	IIC	3, Rahtz 1960–1, Fig. 5	10
30	NE wall	well-defined edges; no foundation over F1	one sherd pottery	IIIA	4,5 ('section DF)	12
31	NW wall	line of wall difficult to distinguish from later rubble; foundation built into F3	pottery (Fig. 13, nos. 27–28)	IIIA	4	12
32	SW wall	follows same line as F38	–	IIIA	4	12
33	floor	clayey soil and small stones below rubble	tip of iron shears blade (Fig. 11, no. 24); pottery	IIIA	4	12
34	drain	stone slabs over F1, cutting through F4	–	IIIA	4,5 (section CD), 6 (section BC)	12

No.	Feature	Description	Notes	Period	Fig.	
35	north part of NW wall	stones laid on bottom course in foundation trench packed with brown clayey soil; outside corner rounded; best piece of masonry on the site, well aligned and dressed and standing to a maximum height of 5 courses	iron hinge pivot and stud (Fig. 11, nos. 18, 22) found below the wall and assigned to IIB; pottery	IIIB	4	12
36	space for wall stud	gap in NW wall filled with black earth on a single flat stone	–	IIIB3	4	16
37	south part of NW wall	stands to a height of 2 courses, packed with clayey soil; over F19 oven and F29	one sherd pottery	IIIB	4	12
38	NE wall	footings of F32 used as a foundation; 1954 section shows it set in a shallow construction trench	–	IIIB	4,5 (section DF) Rahtz, 1960–1, Fig. 5	12
39	post hole for corner post	at junction of F38, and F35, 4 ins diameter, 3 ins deep with wedge stone on one side, filled with dark soil	–	IIIB	4	14
40	SE wall	excavated in 1954, standing to a height of three courses, laid directly on original ground surface	–	IIIB	4	14

No.		Description	Finds	Phase		
41	SW wall	few stones only remaining; packed with green clay, possibly F29	from wall packing jet bead (Fig. 11, no.12) 4th century Roman coin one sherd pottery	IIIB	4	14
42	entrance in SE wall	excavated in 1954, 2 ft 6 ins wide splaying outwards to 5 ft 6 ins, opened onto paved yard with low wall	coin issued c. 1258-72 among paving slabs outside entrance (Rahtz, 1960-1, 68)	IIIB	4	14
43	entrance in NW wall	originally 15 ft 9 ins wide, later narrowed to 4 ft, composed of large flat stones packed with brown clayey soil, resting on 2 ins of brown soil over F14	–	IIIB	4, 6 (section AE)	14
44	yard	outside F43, large worn stones over F14; boundary wall	fr. of vessel glass (Fig. 11, no. 10); tip of iron shears (Fig. 11, no. 25); copper alloy buckle pin (Fig. 11, no. 8); pottery (Fig. 13, nos. 40-48	IIIB	4, 6 (sections AE, BC)	14
45	metalling	stones extending from F44; over F14	fr. hone; stone disc; copper alloy buckle pin (Fig. 11, no. 7); bone whistle (Fig. 11, no. 11); pottery (Fig. 13, nos. 34-39)	IIIB	4, 6 (section AE)	14

No.	Type	Description	Finds	Phase	References	Page
46	hearth	excavated in 1954, composed of stone slabs and ash; hearth area extends to 1954 section and probably to SW wall	clay spindle whorl from base of hearth (Rahtz 1960-1, Fig. 7, no. 6); coin later than c. 1370 and probably before 1400 from ash levels of hearth (Rahtz, 1960-1, 69)	IIIB	4, Rahtz 1960-1, Fig. 5	14
47	timber slot for partition	8–10 ins below F29	–	IIIB	4	14
48	post hole	5 ins below natural, filled with black soil	–	IIIB	4	14
49	floor slabs	large flat stones inside the house, periodically replaced; those inside entrance lie on F29	pottery (Fig. 14, nos. 52–55), including one Roman coarse sherd	IIIB	4,6 (section AE) Rahtz 1960-1 Fig. 5	14
50	floor level	mixed ashy soil with straw impressions; over F29; below F52	cockle and mussel shells; frs. egg shells pottery (Fig. 14, nos. 56–58)	IIIB1	–	14
51	floor slabs	flat stones over F50; below F52	–	IIIB1	4	14
52	clay floor	brown clay 3 ins deep with small stones in the surface; over F50 and F51; below F53 and F58	hone (Fig. 11, no. 1); 3 stone spindle-whorls (Fig. 11, nos. 3–5); iron knife (Fig. 11, no. 14); pottery (Fig. 14, nos. 59–67)	IIIB2	4	16

No.		Description	Finds	Phase	Fig.	Page
53	human cess	grey-green ashy layer mixed with green cessy concretion; covers but mixed up with F52, below F54	pottery (Fig. 15, nos. 68–71)	IIIB2	–	16
54	mortar floor	yellow mortar over F53	fr. hone; pottery (Fig. 15, nos. 72–74)	IIIB4	4	16
55	ditch	in North-West Trench, cutting through F4 metalling; see section for stratigraphy	hone (Fig. 11, no. 2); pottery (Fig. 13, nos. 29–33)	IIIB	4,6 (section AE)	14
56	uncertain	layer of rubble used as a modern vehicle track, possibly medieval in origin	fr. hone; pottery (Fig. 15, nos. 76–79)	?IIIB	4	14
57	extension of NW wall	line of wall built southwards from F35; stones sit on black earth which lies on F5	–	IIIB3	4	16
58	extension of NW wall	line of wall built northwards from F37; packed with clay, stones sit on layer of brown clay with gravel 5 ins thick; over F52	horseshoe tip below wall associated with IIIB2 (Fig. 11, no. 23); pottery, including one sherd samian	IIIB3	4	16
59	realignment of NW wall	stones built alongside F58 and F37 south of the entrance	one sherd pottery	IIIB4	4	16

60	rubble	covering IIIB stone house	IIIB	2 iron knives (Fig. 11, nos. 16–17); pottery (Fig. 15, no. 81) <u>1954 finds (Rahtz 1960–1)</u>; hone from rubble above F42 (Fig. 7, no. 7) iron hasp from chest; rubble on inner side F40 (Fig. 8, no. 1); iron spur (Fig. 8, no. 3); iron key (Fig. 8, no. 4)	–	–
T1	buried 1954 turf and topsoil; layers 2 and 3 in sections		–	fr. hone; iron knife, keyhole escutcheon, scythe blade, sickle blade (Fig. 11, nos. 15, 20, 27, 26); copper alloy patch of sheet metal, thimble (Fig. 11, nos. 6, 9); pottery (Fig. 15, nos. 82–84), including one sherd samian, 4 sherds post-medieval	5 (sections CD, DF), 6 (sections AE, BC)	–
T2	topsoil redeposited during construction layer 1 in sections		–	pottery (Fig. 15, nos. 85–87), including one sherd Iron Age	5 (sections CD, DF), 6 (sections AE, BC)	–

* all pottery is 13th–14th century unless otherwise stated

61

BIBLIOGRAPHY

Algar, D., and Musty, J., 1969, 'Gomeldon', Current Archaeology, 2, no. 14, 87-91.

Barton, K. J., 1960, 'Excavations at Back Hall, Bristol, 1958', Trans. BGAS, 79, Pt. 2, 251-286.

Barton, K.J., 1963, 'A Medieval Pottery Kiln at Ham Green, Bristol', Trans. BGAS, 82, 95-126.

Beresford, M., and Hurst, J. G., eds., 1971, Deserted Medieval Villages, Lutterworth Press, London.

Bolwell, J., 1957, 'Medieval Dovecote, Englishcombe', Med. Arch., 1, 169.

Chatwin, P.B., 1955, 'Brandon Castle, Warwickshire', Trans. BAS, 73, 63-83.

Darby, H. C., and Welldonn Finn, R., eds., 1967, The Domesday Geography of South-West England, University Press, Cambridge.

Dewar, H. S. L., Oct. 1951, 'Discovery of a Lost Medieval Village in Somerset', Archaeological Newsletter, 4, no. 3, 42-43.

Dunning, G. C., 1949, 'Report on the Medieval Pottery from Selsley Common, near Stroud', Trans. BGAS, 68, 22-44.

Ekwall, E., 1960, The Concise Oxford Dictionary of English Place-Names, 4th ed., Clarendon Press, Oxford.

Fowler, P., ed., 1966-1972, C.B.A. Groups XII and XIII Archaeological Review, 1-7, Dept. of Extra-Mural Studies, University of Bristol.

Hawkes, C. F. C., 1959, 'The ABC of the British Iron Age', Antiquity, 33, 170-182.

Hildyard, E. J. W., 1949, 'Further Excavations at Cambokeels in Weardale', Archaeologia Aelina, 27, 177-204.

Hilton, R. H., and Rahtz, P. A., 1966, 'Upton, Gloucestershire, 1959-1964', Trans. BGAS, 85, 70-146.

Jope, E. M., 1952, 'Regional Character in West Country Medieval Pottery', Trans. BGAS, 51, 88-97.

Jope, E. M., and Threlfall, R. I., 1958, 'Excavation of a Medieval Settlement at Beere, North Tawton, Devon', Med. Arch., 2, 112-140.

McCarthy, M. R., 1971, 'Lacock; Naish Hill' (note on kiln excavation), Archaeological Review, ed. P. Fowler, 6, 44.

Megaw, J. V. S., 1968, 'An End-Blown Flute from Medieval Canterbury', Med. Arch., 12, 149-150.

Minter, E. M., 1962-3, 'Hound Tor', (interim note), <u>Med. Arch.</u>, 6-7, 341-343.

Moorhouse, S., 1971, 'Finds from Basing House, Hampshire (<u>c</u>. 1540-1645): Part Two', <u>Post-Medieval Archaeology</u>, 5, 35-76.

Oswald, A., 1962-3, 'Excavation of a Thirteenth-Century Wooden Building at Weoley Castle, Birmingham, 1960-61', <u>Med. Arch.</u>, 6-7, 107-134.

Peacock, D. P. S., 1969, 'A Contribution to the Study of Glastonbury Ware from South-Western Britain', <u>Antiquaries Journal</u>, 49, 41-56.

Rahtz, P. A., 1959, 'Holworth, Medieval Village Excavation 1958', <u>Proc. DNHAS</u>, 81, 127-147.

Rahtz, P. A., 1960, 'Excavation by the Town Wall, Baldwin Street, Bristol, 1957', <u>Trans. BGAS</u>, 79, Pt. 2, 221-250.

Rahtz, P. A., 1960-1, 'Barrow Mead, Bath, Somerset', <u>Proc. SANHS</u>, 105, 61-76.

Rahtz, P. A., 1962-3, 'The Saxon and Medieval Palaces at Cheddar', <u>Med. Arch.</u>, 6-7, 53-66.

Rahtz, P. A., 1964, <u>The Saxon and Medieval Palaces at Cheddar</u>, University of Bristol, M.A. Thesis.

Rahtz, P. A., 1969, 'Upton, Gloucestershire, 1964-68, Second Report', <u>Trans. BGAS</u>, 88, 74-126.

Rahtz, P. A., 1969a, 'Cannington Hillfort 1963', <u>Proc. SANHS</u>, 113, 56-68.

Rahtz, P. A., 1971, 'Excavations on Glastonbury Tor, Somerset, 1964-6', <u>Archaeological Journal</u>, 127, 1-81.

Rahtz, P. A., and Greenfield, E., <u>Excavations at the Chew Valley Lake</u>, H.M.S.O., forthcoming.

PERIODICAL ABBREVIATIONS

<u>Med.Arch.</u>,	<u>Medieval Archaeology</u>
<u>Proc. DNHAS</u>,	<u>Proceedings of the Dorset Natural History and Archaeo-logical Society</u>
<u>Proc. SANHS</u>,	<u>Proceedings of the Somerset Archaeological and Natural History Society</u>
<u>Trans. BAS</u>,	<u>Transactions of the Birmingham Archaeological Society</u>
<u>Trans. BGAS</u>,	<u>Transactions of the Bristol and Gloucestershire Archaeo-logical Society</u>

DOCUMENTARY REFERENCES

C.C.R. 1231	Calendar of Close Rolls, Henry III, 1227-1231
C.F.R. 16	Calendar of Fine Rolls, 1430-1437, 16.
C.I.P.M. 1296	Calendar of Inquisitions Post Mortem, 3.
C.I.P.M. 1315	Calendar of Inquisitions Post Mortem, 5.
F. Aids 1284-5	Feudal Aids, 1284-1431, 5.
F.F. 22	Feet of Fines for Somerset; Somerset Record Society, 1906, 22, ed. E. Green.
K. Quest	Kirby's Quest for Somerset; Somerset Record Society, 1889, 3, ed. F. H. Dickinson.

Plate I: The site from the NE after removal of topsoil

Plate II: The site from the NE after excavation

Plate III.   The NW entrance narrowed, showing paved yard;   Period IIIB4.

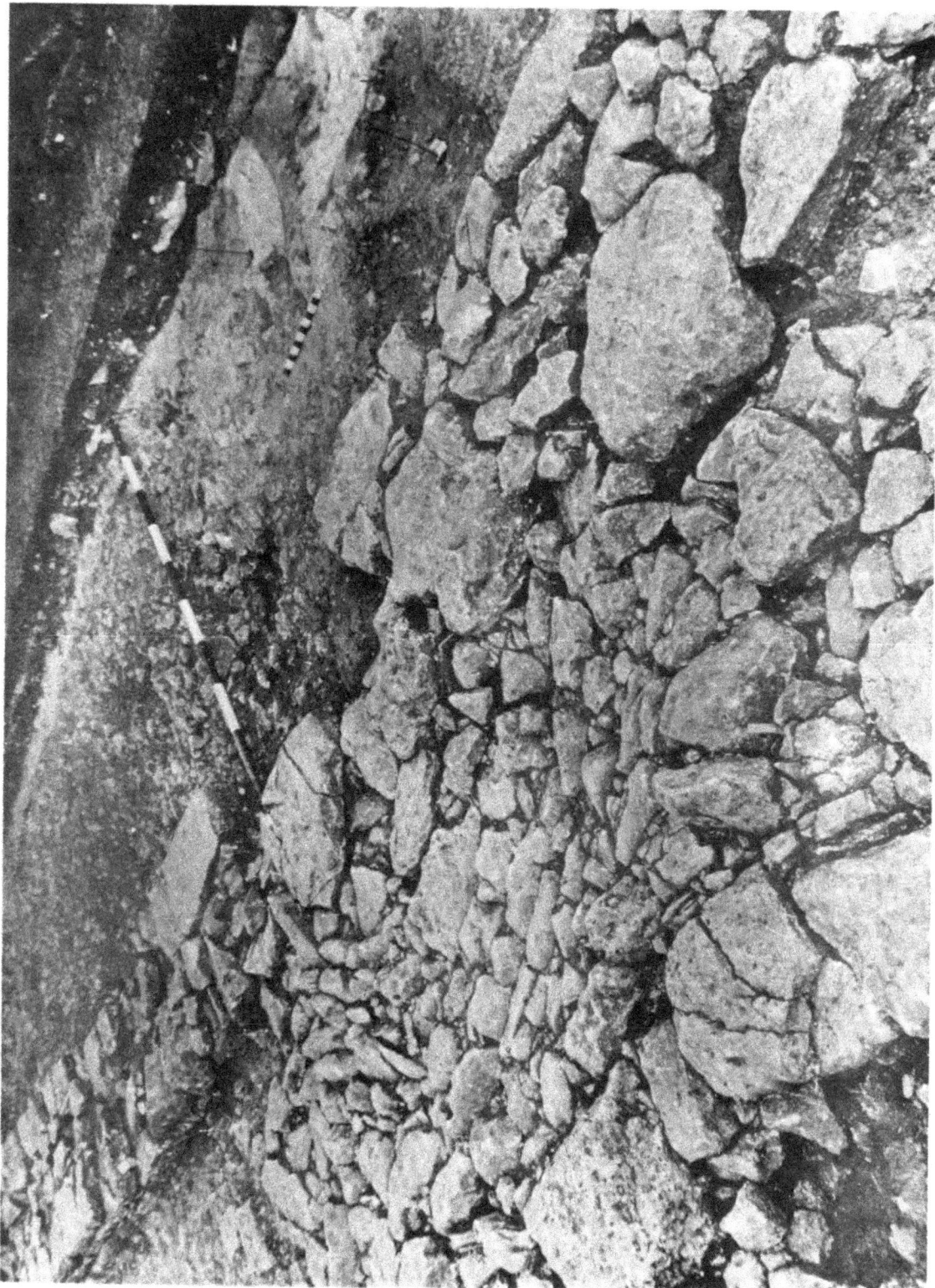

Plate IV: Reconstruction of IIIB stone house in its early phases

www.ingramcontent.com/pod-product-compliance
Lightning Source LLC
Chambersburg PA
CBHW061304270326
41932CB00029B/3472